**Regional Growth and
Water Resource
Investment**

Regional Growth and Water Resource Investment

W. Cris Lewis
Jay C. Andersen
Herbert H. Fullerton
B. Delworth Gardner
Utah State University

Lexington Books
D.C. Heath and Company
Lexington, Massachusetts
Toronto   London

Library of Congress Cataloging in Publication Data

Main entry under title:

Regional growth and water resource investment.

    1. Water resources development. 2. Regional planning. 3. Water resources development—United States. 4. Regional planning—United States. I. Lewis, W. Cris.
HD1691.R44   333.9'1'00973   73-9681
ISBN 0-669-89201-7

Published simultaneously in Canada.

Printed in the United States of America.

International Standard Book Number: 0-669-89201-7

Library of Congress Catalog Card Number: 73-9681

Table of Contents

v

List of Figures

List of Tables

Preface

This book represents the outgrowth of work begun in the summer of 1971 by the authors at Utah State University. The National Water Commission had entered into a contract with the authors to study the way in which investment in water resources might influence the pace and direction of regional economic growth. In a real sense, however, the book is representative of the larger program of water resources research that has a long history at Utah State University.

The question of how such investment might influence growth is an important one, in that allocation of public funds in some cases has been at least partially justified on the expectation that economic growth would be accelerated and, thus, economic welfare increased, by such investment. Unfortunately, both the theoretical and empirical support for such a position are incomplete. It is our goal to broaden the stock of knowledge on this question, and thereby increase the rationality under which these investment decisions are made.

We wish to express our gratitude for the help that we received. Robert P. Collier and Doyle J. Matthews, Deans of the Business and Agriculture Colleges at Utah State University, provided the necessary support to process the manuscript and contributed greatly to the intellectual atmosphere that played a significant role in the writing of the book. Theodore M. Schad, Gary C. Taylor, and John Stierna of the National Water Commission provided direction and constructive criticism during the early stages of the research. Gail Baird and Judy Evans diligently performed the arduous task of editing, typing, and proofreading the manuscript. Norma Thorne and Eleanor Watson assisted with typing. Partial financial support for finishing the manuscript was provided through an institutional development grant [211-D] from the Agency for International Development to Utah State University [Contract AID-csd/2459].

Part I
Framework for Analysis

1 Introduction

The objective of this book is to provide an analysis of the efficacy of water resources investment as a means of achieving regional economic development. Whether this is an appropriate goal for such investment is an interesting question, but it is apparent from many policies and programs that efforts to ameliorate poverty and unemployment are popular enough to be embraced by many political decision makers. Numerous statistical compilations can be used to demonstrate the imbalances in income and wealth among regions. Proposals on how to change these imbalances range from federal monetary and fiscal policies to local income transfers. Water resource development has been suggested and used as one of the tools to redistribute wealth and income. The task here is to evaluate the effectiveness of this approach.

There has been a great deal of research in the fields of study associated with the use and development of water resources.[1] Representatives of virtually every discipline have had something to say about the use of presently available water, the development of new supplies, the impacts of such use on development, etc. The variety of professional backgrounds among the analysts is a natural result of the wide range of services provided by this resource. These include municipal and industrial water supplies, irrigation water for agricultural use, transportation, recreation, flood control, and electric power generation. Not only are the kinds of water resource services numerous, but their development can have diverse and far-ranging effects on the economic, social, and environmental systems in the geographical area of the investment.

Traditionally, the feasibility of a water resource investment has been determined by the one-dimensional benefit-cost criterion. Only if economic benefits, in the present as well as all relevant future time periods (the latter discounted appropriately), exceed the cost of the investment, is the project been deemed feasible. The Water Resources Council has suggested a broader set of guidelines for use in evaluating proposed water resource investments. In these guidelines, it is stated that:[2]

> The overall purpose of water and land resource planning is to reflect society's preferences for attainment of the objectives defined below:
>
> A. To enhance national economic development by increasing the value of the Nation's output of goods and services and improving national economic efficiency.

3

B. To enhance the quality of the environment by the management, conservation, preservation, creation, restoration, or improvement of the quality of certain natural and cultural resources and ecological systems.

C. To enhance regional development through increases in a region's income; increases in employment; distribution of population within and among regions; improvements of the region's economic base and educational, cultural, and recreational opportunities; and enhancement of its environment and other specified components of regional development.

These guidelines give recognition to the concept that water investments have implications that range beyond national economic efficiency considerations. While questions have been raised concerning the appropriateness of certain of these goals,[3] they do represent a broadened scope for feasibility and evaluation studies.

This book will be primarily concerned with the regional development criterion. More specifically, several basic questions will be considered. Do water resource investments influence regional development? If so, what is the process by which such investment causes economic development? What type of project is most likely to promote development in a particular type of region? What tools are especially useful in predicting and measuring the impacts of public investments? What type of accounting framework should be used at the operational level to provide information to the policy or decision maker?

Three primary sources of economic growth at a regional level can be identified: (1) augmented supplies of labor and nonlabor inputs; (2) technological progress, defined as an increase in the maximum level of output attainable with given input quantities; and (3) elimination of resource misallocation through intersectoral and/or interregional shifts of resources to equalize factor returns among those regions and sectors. On an a priori basis, water resource investments might be expected to influence regional growth in all of these sources. For example, an investment that expanded water-based recreational opportunities might accelerate the rate of in-migration to the region, thus increasing available labor supply. The availability of water for agricultural and/or industrial uses could allow radically different production processes that would significantly reduce per unit production costs. The construction of a navigable channel through a primarily low-income agricultural area might be expected to induce the location of manufacturing industries that produce water-transportable goods. Labor would flow from the agricultural sector to the higher wage manufacturing jobs, thus creating an increase in regional income. These conjectures are subject to both theoretical and empirical verification, however. A thorough investigation is needed into the way regions grow, the reaction of firms and individuals to increased or improved water resources, and the possibility that other investments might accomplish the same results at a lower cost.

Clarification is needed on regional vis-à-vis national perspective. Some regional development merely represents a shifting of activity from one place to another. Although the region on the receiving end of the act benefits to the extent regional employment and income rise, this may be exactly offset by declines in the other region, so that the net gain for the national economy is zero (or negative if the relocation costs are taken into consideration). In making recommendations for improving the analysis in a comprehensive program to develop the nation's water resources, it is essential that a national perspective be adopted, especially if national resources are used in financing and repayment. This viewpoint will be used throughout this book. Consideration must be given to the effect that water investment might have on the productivity of the other resources in the region, both human and nonhuman, and not merely on whether such an investment will cause an interregional shift of activities. Admittedly, the local Chamber of Commerce or State Industrial Development Department may logically adopt a narrower point of view.

Two questions might be raised at this point. Should the federal government be involved in efforts to expand the rate of economic development in some regional economies? And what is the rationale for government rather than the private sector providing most water and water-related services? Although these questions are somewhat peripheral to the primary theme of this book, a brief discussion of them will provide a useful background.

A number of arguments have been used to justify reliance on the public sector for ownership and development of the nation's water resources. First, the water industry has characteristics of a public utility in that it would be inefficient to have competing systems for water delivery. That is, the water industry has traits of a natural monopoly. Second, it has been asserted that the massive capital requirements of the larger projects can only be met by the public sector. Third, the interdependencies among users of the resource suggest the need for some type of social control over use and withdrawal. Clearly the use of water at one site can have significant implications for downstream users. Pollution is a good example. The existence of externalities almost assures that a competitive market will fail to achieve an optimal allocation of the resource. Fourth, in many cases it would be impractical for a private firm to charge the beneficiaries of the development. An obvious example is a flood control project wherein protection cannot be made selective—everyone will benefit whether they pay or not. However, in other cases, such as in a recreation-oriented project where access to the resource could be controlled, inclusion of only those who pay may be quite easily accomplished.

Whether there exists a rationale for federal involvement in the development of lagging regions depends on one's perception of how the economic system should influence the spatial allocation of economic activity.[4] Acceptance of the national demand theory, which asserts that competitive forces working through the market will always create an optimal spatial arrangement of economic activity, would suggest a very small role for the federal sector, possibly

one designed only to ease transfer problems by offering limited and temporary
financial assistance to the individuals affected. Alternatively, the theory of
planned adjustment argues that competitive forces do not create optimal distributions of economic activity, and, therefore, national economic efficiency
requires some form of intervention by the public sector. As the federal government has the necessary resources and is not constrained by state and local
political boundaries, it is the logical candidate for the primary role in developing
regional economies. The acceptance of regional development as one of the goals
to be achieved by water resource investment suggests an acceptance of the
latter theory by federal policy makers.

One element of the rationale for the planned adjustment theory is based on
the assertion that large-scale shifts of human resources from the smaller rural
communities to the large metropolitan areas of the country are inefficient when
measured from a social point of view. The small cities and rural areas which are
the source of migrants in this "rural-urban" population shift are often left with
a redundant stock of both private and social capital. Such capital must be
duplicated to serve the needs of the increased population in the metropolis.
There is waste of social capital because the individual decision to migrate is based
on an assessment of private, rather than social costs and benefits. Some analysts
claim that external diseconomies, such as those associated with congestion and
pollution, are sufficiently great that the social costs associated with further
rural-urban population movements are greatly in excess of private costs (and
social benefits), and that federal programs to slow or even reverse this population
shift are in order.[5]

While a more detailed discussion of these ideas would be too far afield, it
is essential to have some background for the justification for federal involvement
in regional economic growth. Although the arguments, pro and con, are still
being discussed, it is clear that a sizeable federal effort in this direction is being
made, and there is no indication of any slowdown in the rate of development
of new programs and growth of expenditures. The establishment of regional
development commissions, economic development districts, and requirements
on government agencies that they procure from small firms is evidence of the
commitment. Whether this is because of explicit acceptance of the planned
adjustment concept, or is based simply on equity grounds, or, possibly, a mere
random occurrence, is not particularly important at the moment. However, since
the federal government is engaging, and will almost surely continue to engage in
programs designed to boost economic development in regions, it is important to
ask if the development of a region's water resources offers an effective and
predictable tool for accomplishing that end, and, if so, under what circumstances?

Perhaps the biggest obstacle facing the development of a rational water
resource investment program is the view, common in many circles, that water is a
"special" resource, and, therefore, the economics principles widely used in the
pricing and allocation of other resources are not applicable here. This view

apparently stems from the unique life-giving image sometimes ascribed to water. The terms "water shortage" or "water short" region appear frequently, and are generally followed by proposals to alleviate the "shortage" through some type of investment designed to increase available supply. Water shortage is invariably defined as an excess of quantity demanded over available supply at some given artificial price. Generally, no consideration is given to allowing a rationing of the limited water supply by using the price mechanism as a rationing device. The position taken in this book is that many "water shortages" are artificial and arise from the administrative pricing of available water, and that there is nothing very mystical or different about this resource which negates the usefulness of sound economic principles.

An inseparable part of this problem is the conventional notion that there exists a set of requirements for water for the various uses (i.e., agriculture, industry, consumers, etc.) rather than a set of demand functions. A "requirement" suggests that a given quantity of water is required per unit of output, rather than that the quantity of water used per unit of output is variable depending on the price of the water input. The notion of water requirements is the antithesis of the concept of a flexible production function that allows the substitution of one input for another. The concept of "requirements" is rejected and the term "water demand" substituted, to reflect the fact that water and other resources can be used in each other's place, and that there is a difference in amount taken by users depending on whether the resource is economically scarce or plentiful. More will be said on this subject later. In this book water will be viewed as a resource, admittedly having certain special characteristics, and it will be studied, analyzed, and valued using the same principles that are applied to other resources. Food, clothing, medicine, etc., are highly essential, but, generally, market forces determine the price and allocation of these scarce resources among competing uses. Within a market economy, the use of emotional tenets for pricing and allocating water can be expected to result in an inferior or suboptimal resource allocation.

The idea that market forces should, in large part, determine the pricing and allocation of water resources does not imply that such resources should be provided only by the private sector. Water does have certain characteristics that, under many circumstances, lend it more amenable to development by the public sector. Thus, the concepts of opportunity costs, resource demands, and marginal principles of pricing and allocation are relevant and applicable for public development, allocation, and pricing of water.

This book is organized into three major parts. The first is devoted to the development of a framework within which an economic analysis of water investment can be logically evaluated. The important concepts to be developed include regional delineation, the theory of regional growth, and the measurement of economic welfare and growth. The second part considers the role of water resource investment in the regional growth process, and constitutes the heart of the analysis. The discussion ranges from an examination of the characteristics and notions of the water resource to its role in industrial activity. Also considered is the possible developmental sequence that follows water resource investments. In the third part, an accounting framework for analyzing water investment is outlined, and alternative quantitative techniques for estimating and predicting the development impacts are reviewed and evaluated. Important summary statements and conclusions are offered in this final part.

Notes

1. An indication of the water-oriented research literature is given by the recently published, two part *Water Resources Research Catalog, Volume 7.* (Washington, D.C.: Water Resources Scientific Information Center, Office of Water Resources Research, U.S. Department of the Interior, 1972).
2. Water Resources Council. "Proposed Principles and Standards for Planning Water and Related Land Resources," *Federal Register.* Washington, D.C.: National Archives of the United States. XXXVI, 245 (December 21, 1971) 24145.
3. For examples, see: Daniel W. Bromley, "Social Goals, Water Resource Development, and the Water Resources Council: A Critical Assessment." *Proceedings*, 44th Annual Meeting, Western Agricultural Economics Association, Squaw Valley, California. (July 25–27, 1971). pp. 134–139. Wade H. Andrews, et al., *Identification and Measurement of Quality of Life Elements in Planning for Water Resources Development: An Exploratory Study*, Research Report No. 2, prepared for the Bureau of Reclamation, U.S. Department of the Interior. (Logan, Utah: Institute for Social Science Research on Natural Resources, Utah State University. April, 1972.)
4. See: Gordon C. Cameron. *Regional Economic Development: The Federal Role* (Baltimore: The Johns Hopkins Press. 1970).
5. There is some disagreement on this point. One economist argues that economies of scale and agglomeration in production may be sufficiently significant, that it might be rational to subsidize in-migration to the cities, so as to bring about increases in average product per worker and in the wage rate. See William Alonso, "The Economics of Urban Size," *Regional Science Association Papers, European Congress, London, 1970.* Philadelphia: The Regional Science Association, in cooperation with the Department of Regional Science, Wharton School, University of Pennsylvania. XXVL (1971) 67–83.

2 Regional Delineation for Water Investment Planning and Analysis

The identification of appropriate areas for use in planning and evaluating water resources investments is a critical first step in the analysis. In general, the social, economic, and political implications of public investment decisions have differential impacts, depending on regional characteristics. Arbitrarily-defined political boundaries, individual resource availabilities and requirements, and differential rates of adjustment in overcoming structural problems are unique to any area. These elements tend to increase the difficulty and often the necessity of generating regionally specific, but consistent and meaningful information on which to base policy decisions.

A review of agency feasibility and framework studies suggests a strong hydrologic-engineering orientation in the delineation of regions. Most water resource development projects have utilized a river basin or project service area approach as the basic spatial unit. In such cases, measures of water volume and flow are the important regional delineators, often to the exclusion of such equally important flow variables as labor and commodity movements. The latter often exhibit only random correspondence to the hydrologic boundaries. Since the primary criterion for identifying a "good" water investment is a benefit-cost test and further proposals are to include regional growth and equity considerations, it seems appropriate that the basic spatial unit for analysis be defined primarily from an economic point of view. In virtually all cases such units could be combined to conform to relevant hydrologic areas where that would be useful.

There are numerous constraints that must be recognized in any attempt to define the appropriate area for assessing water development impacts. Specific considerations include the following questions. Does the unit have a sufficient job-access orientation to provide for meaningful employment, income, and well-being of people considerations? Is the unit characterized by a degree of economic automony (i.e., it is closed with respect to enough activities and flows) sufficient to distinguish it from neighboring regions? Can the individual units be aggregated with others to form units large enough to capture the full spatial impacts of the investment or to conform to hydrologic or other boundaries? Can current and historical data essential for economic analysis be readily obtained from existing sources?

Another problem arises when considering the effects of multiple-purpose projects. It is likely that the extent of areas influenced by the several purposes of such a project—recreation, power, etc.—will differ significantly. Conceivably, a set of different regional units, one for each purpose, could be identified. More

9

useful, however, would be one set of regions, to be used in all analyses, integrated into an accounting framework wherein the differential area impact of the several services can be easily identified.

These are but a few of the items that must be given consideration. Clearly, no unit will be best in all respects; what is needed is one that comes closest to meeting the various requirements. In the next section of the chapter three general types of regional delineation will be reviewed. In the last section the concept of the functional economic area (FEA) will be considered, and a recommendation made that, because it best meets the requirements outlined above, the FEA should be adopted for general use in the economic evaluation of water resources as well as other public projects.

Types of Regional Classifications

Regions can be classified on the basis of policy orientation, homogeneity, and nodality.[1] Policy regions are usually coincident with the boundaries of such political entities as cities, counties, and states. Within such regions there exist both administrative capacity and legal basis for action on a wide range of economic as well as noneconomic problems. A fundamental problem with most policy regions is that their arbitrarily defined boundaries render them useless for purposes of economic analysis or planning. In cases where some type of economic or social rationale was used in the delineation, it has been rendered obsolete by technological change.[a]

The result of a spatial divergence between political units and meaningful economic regions is obvious. Officials in the component counties of a larger economic region will not be in a position to implement policies that will have a significant impact on the regional economy. To some extent this problem is being overcome by the formation of multicounty organizations (e.g., councils of governments and regional planning commissions) which are governed by city and county officials from the various political jurisdictions of the region, but are in a better position than smaller jurisdictional units to make meaningful plans, policies, and programs for the entire regional economy. At least one federal government program aimed at regional economic development has recognized the limitations of existing political units in influencing the pace of such development. The Economic Development Administration (EDA) has established a number of multicounty economic development districts to coordinate planning for social investment in an attempt to increase the level of welfare in relatively low income areas.

---

[a]For example, county boundaries in some states were established so that any resident could travel from his home to the county seat and back by horse and buggy within one day. The substitution of the automobile and interstate highway for the horse and the dirt road have made such a delineation almost completely useless for purposes of economic analysis.

The homogeneity concept classifies regions as being together if they share one or more physical, social, economic, or other characteristics. For example, ethnic neighborhoods within large cities might constitute a set of regions. Per capita income levels are often used to distinguish between different areas of the country. In dealing with water resources, river basins have been identified as the appropriate units for study. As suggested above, however, a regional delineation based on standard homogeneity criteria is suboptimal for assessing economic development impacts. A project may supply municipal and industrial water to a city characterized by above average per capita income and also irrigation water to a low income agricultural area. As these areas may have significant economic linkages, to classify them as distinct regions because of a divergence in income levels would be a mistake.

In the nodal region, attention is focused on the center, usually the largest city, and its interrelations with smaller cities and rural areas in the region. These regions are usually composed of heterogeneous elements having strong functional linkages. For example, many multicounty regions are characterized by a central city where manufacturing is the dominant activity, a rural area where agriculture forms the industrial base, and a set of smaller cities that act as service centers for the population in the nearby rural areas. Generally, these regions are closed with respect to labor force commuting patterns, distribution of retail goods and services, and/or some communications media. In the nodal region a more than proportionate share of the region's economic activity takes place at the center, as flows of people, goods, and communications tend to concentrate in the focal or central city.

Labor markets are useful approximations to nodal regions. The commuting radius to the largest city in the region internalizes its home-to-work trips and spatially captures most of the retail and services expenditures of the region's residents. Family income is largely earned and expended within the labor market and this region contains most of the households that consume public services offered by the central city. A labor market is often the geographical basis for regional planning commissions concerned with coordinating the development of transportation facilities among constituent counties. Also, it may provide an appropriate region for consolidating certain governmental services.

For purposes of identifying and measuring economic impacts of public investment projects, it is essential that functional linkages within and among regions be given explicit consideration. If information concerning the implications of induced changes due to public intervention is to be viewed in a meaningful context, area units which recognize regional and sectoral diversity, as well as the internal and external linkages of these units, must be considered. As the primary or first round impacts of such investment are usually manifest in a given geographical area, the nodal region or some variant thereof appears to be the logical basic unit for analysis. As water resource investments are generally made by nonlocal governmental units, although often local contributions to funding are involved, the policy regions would offer few, if any, advantages. Likewise, the homogeneity delineation, as commonly used, would not offer any advantage in such analyses.

The Functional Economic Area

Fox's articulation of the functional economic area (FEA) concept provides an excellent example of the use of heterogeneous nodal regions in economic analysis.[2] He states that a people- and job-oriented region is better suited to understanding spatial economic organization and changes therein than are other, more traditional delineations. A basis for defining these "ideal" regions is derived from recognizing that: essential services and a major share of regional employment are offered in the central or nodal city; the perimeter of the spatial unit within which most people movements are made is defined by the maximum time a resident will spend commuting to work (this is estimated to be about 60 minutes); and there are scale economies and minimum thresholds in the production of certain goods and services, suggesting that the nodal city must be in excess of some minimum size in order to be viable.

Essentially, the functional economic area is a multicounty labor market (i.e., the area is closed with respect to commuting patterns) usually centered on a focal city of 25,000 or more inhabitants.[b] Criteria of metropolitan character such as population density and size, which are used in designating standard metropolitan statistical areas (SMSA's), are discarded in favor of more basic economic integration and/or people-job criteria. Where people locate themselves and tend to concentrate commuting patterns around a nodal city, there exists an FEA.

Fox argues that although the landscape characteristics of many of these FEA's differ from those usually associated with a city, these FEA's should be viewed as spatially-extended urban areas. The low density rural area is merely the site of one of the export industries (i.e., agriculture) of this "extended" city, and the smaller peripheral towns act as service centers for noncentral city residents in much the same way as do suburban shopping centers in a large metropolitan area.

Not only is the FEA more applicable in economic analysis, it is also more comprehensive geographically than is the traditional SMSA system. The system of FEA's as identified by Berry, et al., [3] covers more than 80 percent of the

---

[b]This original estimate of 25,000 as a minimum size for a central city was revised downward as it was found that in some areas, particularly in the Midwest and Rocky Mountain areas, substantially smaller cities were, in fact, the focus of multicounty labor markets. Spencer, Iowa (population 10,278); Rawlins, Wyoming (7,855); and Miles City, Montana (9,023) are cases in point.

land area and 96 percent of the population of the United States.[c] It is recognized that rigid use of the existing FEA system would exclude substantial portions of some states, particularly in the intermountain area. The intent of the recommendation that FEA's be applied generally in water investment analysis centers on the obvious advantages of using FEA or FEA-type areas to provide a rational spatial context for development analysis. As it is important that the area delineation exhaust all relevant areas, some modification of the strict FEA definitions must be made so that the very low population counties not linked to a central city (and, therefore, not included in any FEA) can be taken into account. Use might be made of other delineations, such as state planning areas, to complement the FEA method. In practical applications it has been shown that little analytical value is lost by defining FEA's to include only entire counties; this is an easy way to identify FEA's and greatly reduces the data collection problem.

The FEA concept is gaining wide acceptance. There is indication that the Bureau of the Census may begin reporting some data on an FEA basis. State and other federal government agencies are using FEA type areas for administrative and other purposes. Zip Code areas used by the United States Postal Service tend to correspond with urban commuting fields and, hence, with FEA's. With some exceptions, multicounty units used by the Economic Development Administration provide close approximations to FEA's. Similarly, recommendations of national church groups, extension services, and groups charged with making recommendations for modernizing local government point to the necessity of viewing their activities within a context having the essential features of the FEA's.

An application of the use of FEA-type areas in water oriented research is found in the Susquehanna study.[4] In that study, the project area or the physical drainage basin of the Susquehanna River, consisting of 49 counties in four states, was divided into eight economic subareas based on labor commuting patterns and retail and wholesale trade flows.

> Subregions were selected that minimized commuting from one subregion to another. By selecting subregions in this way, the growth of economic activity (employment) in one subregion has a minimum effect on that of other subregions. This effect is further minimized by attempting to assure that the subregions selected are also retail and

---

[c]Based on 1960 census data on commuting patterns, a matrix was developed that associated workers living in 43,000 census tracts with 4,300 possible central workplace areas. After identifying 305 dominant central county workplace locations as FEA centers, counties surrounding each one were included in the FEA of that central county, if the proportion of resident workers commuting to that central county exceeded the proportion commuting to alternative central counties. As an indication of the magnitude of this task, the reporting booklets for commuting data within SMSA's alone comprise a 40-foot pile of computer output paper.

wholesale trading areas. This ensures that income by an employee working and residing within one subregion is not largely spent in another. Thus, the regionalization procedures were designed to yield fairly autonomous economic areas with a minimum of economic interdependence.[5]

If the Susquehanna project is any indication, it is likely that there will be significant differences among subregions in measures of economic structure and performance such as per capita income, the unemployment rate, and industry composition.[d] Assessment of economic differentials among subregions is critical, as the effects of water investment will differ, not only among project areas, but among the several subregions of a specific project area.

In a recent study, FEA's were compared to several alternative delineations to determine the area sensitivity of selected economic and social measures.[6] Each of the sets compared was exhaustive in the sense that a summation for any given measure over similarly defined regions would result in a total for the state. It was found that measures of relative variation by area type varied inversely with region size. For example, the coefficient of variation for per capita income among a set of 16 FEA's was considerably larger than for the set of 6 hydrologically-defined river basins. In subbasins defined to include all FEA's whose central cities were within the hydrologic basin, coefficients of variation for developmental indicators were larger in 17 or 22 cases than in their hydrologically-defined counterparts. A similar comparison between FEA's and these hydrologic basins showed greater relative variation for FEA's in 21 of 22 categories.

This suggests that important information may be lost when only hydrologic area units are used for assessing economic and social impacts of water development. Perhaps even more important, those indicators of regional development which require resident access, such as employment opportunity, residentiary services, and some amenities, cannot be realistically compared among regional units larger than or on different bases than FEA's. To do so would ignore time and distance costs which would cause effective wage rates to be unattractive, and the prices of essential services and amenities to be prohibitively high.

The FEA delineation yields a set of relatively autonomous regions. The inter-FEA linkages are generally confined to only a subset of the producing sectors and commuting across FEA lines is minimized. Thus, the FEA provides a reasonably stable and independent planning unit. It provides a useful context for viewing developmental indicators, since an essential part of its delineation criteria are based on resident access to employment and a minimal range of services. Some weaknesses are inherent for programming and policy application if the FEA's are defined in the most rigorous fashion, because FEA boundaries

---

[d] As an indication of the differences in economic structure among those regions, the unemployment rate ranged from 3.2 percent to 9.2 percent, per capita income from $1,500 to $2,100, and percentage of employment in agriculture from 1.5 to 8.9 percent.

will not, in general, coincide with recognized governmental units; but this should not be a major obstacle to sound economic evaluation and analysis.

As the focus of this book is on the regional economic development implications of water investments, we submit that the use of functional economic areas provides the essential building blocks for constructing an appropriate regional context. Since a region should be large enough so that virtually all of the area in which there are significant impacts will be included, the water investment project area may include several FEA's. By using these building blocks, the differential impacts on the component FEA's in the project area can be easily identified, and the total effects readily estimated by summing across all relevant FEA's. Identification of changes in economic flows among FEA's is facilitated by the limited number of inter-FEA linkages. The advantages of the functional economic area delineation for economic research of many types clearly outweigh the few drawbacks. Throughout the rest of this book, the FEA will be considered as the primary spatial unit for economic analysis.

Notes

1. J.R. Meyer, "Regional Economics: A Survey," *American Economic Review*, LII, 1 (March, 1963) 19–54.

2. Karl A. Fox and T.K. Kumar, "Delineating Functional Economic Areas," in Iowa State University Center for Agricultural and Economic Development, eds., *Research and Education for Area Development* (Ames: Iowa State University Press, 1966) pp. 13–55.

3. Brian J.L. Berry, Peter G. Goheen, and Harold Goldstein, *Metropolitan Area Definition: A Re-Evaluation of Concept and Practice*, working paper No. 28, U.S. Department of Commerce (Washington, D.C., 1968).

4. H.R. Hamilton, et al., *Systems Simulation for Regional Analysis: An Application to River-Basin Planning* (Cambridge, Mass.: The MIT Press, 1969).

5. *Ibid.*, p. 118.

6. Herbert H. Fullerton, "An Economic Simulation Model for Development and Planning" (unpublished Ph.D. dissertation, Iowa State University, 1971).

3 Regional Growth Theory and Water Resource Investment

Introduction

In addition to the use of appropriately-defined regions, analysis of the economic impacts of water resource investments requires a basic understanding of the regional growth process. Although considerable research effort has been expended on the development of regional growth models, a construct of general applicability and widespread acceptance among regional economists has yet to be developed.[1] The continued dependence on the outdated and somewhat unrealistic export-base theory is an indication of the rather undeveloped state of this field. The problem is a serious one, in that some public investment decisions are based largely on the economic effects expected to result from the installation of an incremental unit of social capital, which would supposedly augment the export base of a region. Without a rather complete understanding of the growth process, such benefits are likely to be misestimated. Some public investments have not had the expected impacts because they were based on assumptions regarding the regional growth process that were erroneous. Others were not begun because existing theory and procedures were not capable of predicting the primary and secondary impacts on the regional economy.

Focusing on growth in one of a set of regions in an open economy introduces several complicating dimensions that tend not to be given explicit consideration in national level growth models. Interregional flows of goods, services, and capital tend to be of greater relative importance than are similar flows among nations. Depending on the area delineation used, regions often are highly specialized in the production of particular commodities or services, and, therefore, a significant proportion of domestic output is exported. Similarly, a large share of domestic consumption and production requirements must be imported. There may also be substantial flows of capital among regions, depending on the saving habits of the region's residents, the size and diversity of financial institutions in the area, and domestic capital requirements.

Interregional movement of human resources presents another important dimension that must be included in regional growth analysis. Such migration is often linked to differential opportunities for employment among the several regions, and, therefore, has important implications for individual welfare considerations. Empirical evidence suggests that labor tends to be less mobile than some forms of capital, and that areas of high unemployment, although typically characterized by out-migration, tend to remain such over periods as long as several generations. Economic theory would predict that differentials in wage and unemployment rates would cause equilibrating movements of people from low-wage, high-unemployment areas to regions characterized by high wages and/or tight labor markets. Such movement is observed, but has not succeeded in eliminating these differentials. There are several possible explanations for this. Individuals may prefer the lower income in the home region to the uncertainty, discomfort, and cost of moving to the "advanced" area. Essentially, this is an assertion that people attempt to maximize utility rather than income and are risk-averters rather than risk-seekers. In addition, the possibility that technical progress and scale economies are concentrated in growing regions, could result in the demand function for labor (and possibly capital as well) increasing more than enough to offset increases in the factor supply function. Such a situation could result in continuing wage (and profit) differentials among regions despite the existence of equilibrating factor movements. The speed of factor movement reaction to such differentials is critical in the determination of relative factor prices among regions.

These interregional flows, coupled with diversity among regions with regard to resource endowments, spatial location vis-à-vis markets and raw material sources, climatic conditions, etc., suggest that regional growth models must be somewhat more intricate and detailed than are models developed for a larger, closed economy. Furthermore, the paucity of data on a regional basis, especially on interregional flows of goods, services, labor, and capital, hinders the testing and verification of these regional constructs.

These factors help to explain why regional growth theory is not well developed. Although existing models do cast light on the growth process, many questions still remain unanswered. It is against this background that an assessment of the economic effects of one class of public investment will be made. This review of growth theory proceeds with the objective of identifying the important contributions of each model to an understanding of the process by which regions grow or decline, and the implications of each model for predicting and explaining the impacts of water resource investments.

A comprehensive theory of regional growth, one that would be useful for policy-making purposes, should be capable of identifying the sources of economic growth and the interactions among them, with particular emphasis on those sources amenable to policy manipulation. It should be able to predict the magnitude and direction of interregional and intersectoral factor movements and the effect of such movements on relative factor prices, both among regions and sectors. Ideally the processes involved in such reallocations would be shown explicitly within the context of a dynamic model. The regional growth theory should also be capable of predicting the growth impact of various types of investments. It would be very useful, although perhaps too much to expect, to be able to predict the impacts of alternative types of water investments on employment, income, population, etc., within the project area. The theory should be able to demonstrate the effects of changes in technology and demand changes exogenous to the region on the equilibrium growth path, and determine the necessary conditions for steady-state growth of income, output, and employment.

No existing growth model exhibits all of these characteristics, but these idealistic capabilities provide a useful guide for evaluating the current state of the art. It will also become apparent that existing models are too aggregative to be more than indicative about the differential impacts of specific types of investment. Each model discussed below, however, does have important implications for our analysis, and these will be emphasized.

In the following review, regional growth models are categorized in the following way: (1) aggregate Keynesian-type models where demand factors dominate (the export-base model is used as the primary example); (2) macroeconomic models concentrating on factor supplies and quality, technical progress, and elimination of resource misallocation; and (3) models which use industrial composition to explain differential growth among regions. In each of these sections one or more models will be developed and the implications of the model for predicting the growth impacts of water investment will be examined. In a concluding section, empirical research on the sources of economic growth is reviewed.

Demand-Oriented Models of Regional Growth

Although the export or economic base model [2] is probably the best known and most widely-used regional growth model, it is seriously deficient in that it recognizes only one source of growth—increased demand for regional exports. The theory asserts that the region's basic activities (i.e., those which involve the sale of goods and services to consumers whose source of payment comes from extraregional sources) form the basis for the development of all other (nonbasic) activities. Exogenous changes in demand for output from a subset of the region's industries, arising from outside the region, are the ultimate source of change in total regional employment with population and labor force adjusting passively. Generally, basic or export activity is concentrated in the manufacturing, extractive, and agricultural sectors.

For illustrative purposes, two variants of this model will be reviewed. The first, which approaches regional economic change by identifying the basic/nonbasic employment dichotomy and then tracing exogenous changes in the former through to induced changes in the latter, is useful in explaining the key features of the theory. The second variant, which analyzes income and product flows in a multiregional context, extends the theory as well as making evident some of its shortcomings.

Total regional employment (E) is identically equal to the sum of employment in the basic (E_b) and nonbasic (E_n) sectors:

$$E \equiv E_b + E_n \tag{3-1}$$

Basic employment is assumed to be an exogenous variable in that it depends on those extraregional forces that determine export demand,

$$E_b = E_b^0 \tag{3-2}$$

while nonbasic employment is an increasing function of basic employment[a],

$$E_n = \alpha_1 + \beta_1 E_b^0, \tag{3-3}$$

where $\beta_1 > 0$
Solving for total employment yields

$$E = \alpha_1 + (1 + \beta_1) E_b^0 \tag{3-4}$$

where the derivative of E with respect to E_b, $(1 + \beta_1)$ is the total employment multiplier associated with a change in basic employment. β_1 would be interpreted as a nonbasic employment multiplier.

The model is completed by adding an equation where population (P) in the region is a function of total employment,

$$P = \alpha_2 + \beta_2 E \tag{3-5}$$

Substituting (3-4) into (3-5) yields an equation for population as a function of basic employment only,

$$P = \alpha_2 + \beta_2 \alpha_1 + \beta_2 (1 + \beta_1) E_b^0 \tag{3-6}$$

where $\beta_2(1 + \beta_1)$ would be considered a population-basic employment multiplier.

Any change in the region's employment and population must stem from changes in the one exogenous variable, E_b^0. Strictly speaking, this is not a growth model, although it is commonly referred to as such. In a rather trivial sense, a growth model can be developed by assuming basic employment to be increasing at a constant rate r,

$$E_{bt} = E_b^0 e^{rt} \tag{3-7}$$

---

[a]Although the actual relationship may not be linear, as described here, alternative nonlinear forms of Equation (3-3) would not change the important conclusions to be derived.

where t indexes time periods. Under this condition, growth rates for total employment and population will equal that for basic employment. If functions (3-4) and (3-6) were nonlinear, the growth rates would differ among the three variables.

This model has some very obvious shortcomings. First, there would appear to be no basis for the omission of autonomous spending other than exports. In many regions, autonomous components of consumption, investment, and government expenditures would be significant, perhaps more so that the region's exports. Second, the possibility of technical progress[b] is omitted entirely from consideration. Either this factor is not considered as a potential source of growth, or it is of such minor importance compared to export volume, that it need not be given explicit consideration. Third, it is implicitly assumed that the demand functions for both labor and commodities are perfectly inelastic, while the labor supply schedule is infinitely elastic. Increased demand for commodities, ostensibly arising from increased export demand, has no effect on factor price—it influences only the quantity demanded of the factors involved.[3] Fourth, the assumption that export demand is exogenous cannot be maintained when interregional linkages are explicitly identified. In the second variant, developed below, it is evident that exports of one region must be dependent on income levels in all other regions, and, therefore, the former must be endogenous. Finally, the identification of a region's economic base involves difficult measurement problems. Methods for dividing regional activity into basic and nonbasic components include direct survey and questionnaire techniques, as well as indirect estimation methods, such as location quotients and minimum requirements. While all of these techniques have certain problems associated with their use, the measurement problem is thought to be of a lower order when compared to the more fundamental weaknesses discussed above.

The development of a multiregion income determination model should cast additional light on both the economic interrelationships among regions and some of the weaknesses in the export-base theory. Consider an m region economy where regional income is the sum of consumption (C_i), investment (I_i), exports (X_i), and government spending in the region (G_i) less imports into the region (M_i):

$$Y_i = C_i + I_i + X_i - M_i + G_i, \qquad i = 1, \ldots, m \qquad (3-8)$$

Consumption of regional output is a linear function of regional income,

$$C_i = a_i + c_i Y_i \qquad (3-9)$$

---

[b]Technical progress will be defined to mean either an increase in the maximum level of output attainable with given input levels, or a reduction in the inputs required to produce a given level of output.

and investment and government spending are determined exogenously,

$$I_i = \bar{I}_i \tag{3-10}$$

$$G_i = \bar{G}_i \tag{3-11}$$

Imports to a region are assumed to be a linear function of regional income,

$$M_i = \sum_{\substack{j=1 \\ j \neq i}}^{m} \mu_{ji} Y_i \tag{3-12}$$

where μ_{ji} is the marginal propensity of region i to import from region j, and, therefore, export volume from the ith region must equal the sum of imports from region i to all other regions j:

$$X_i = \sum_{\substack{j=1 \\ j \neq i}}^{m} \mu_{ij} Y_j \tag{3-13}$$

If import volume is dependent on income, as generally assumed, then imports must be an endogenous variable. In a closed multiregion economy, total imports must be identically equal to total exports,

$$\sum_{i=1}^{m} M_i \equiv \sum_{i=1}^{m} X_i \tag{3-14}$$

and, therefore, if the former is endogenous then so must be the latter. Rather than change in export volume causing changes in income, it is more likely that the causal sequence is just the reverse. It would appear that exports are determined by other factors rather than the exogenous factor, i.e., increased export volume is a residual effect of growth and not a primary causal factor.

Solving equation system (3-8) - (3-13) for income yields.

$$Y_i = \cfrac{S_i + \sum_{\substack{j=1 \\ j \neq i}}^{m} \mu_{ij} Y_j}{1 - (c_i - \sum_{\substack{j=1 \\ j \neq i}}^{m} \mu_{ji})} \tag{3-15}$$

where S_i is the sum of exogenous spending components,

$$S_i = a_i + \bar{I}_i + \bar{G}_i$$

A change in regional income can be caused by a change in any autonomous expenditure in the region (i.e., a_i, $\bar{I}_i$, $+ \bar{G}_i$); a change in any of these components in another region, say j, which will cause Y_j to change, setting off a series of changes in the volume and pattern of interregional trade; and/or changes in any of the parameters of the system.

Although the analysis to this point has been generally critical of the export-base theory of regional growth, it must be admitted that forces external to the region can have significant impacts on the regional economy, but from a national viewpoint it is quite clear that expansion of regional trade is not a viable policy tool for stimulating long-run growth in the component regions. A pragmatic view of this concept is taken by Richardson: [4]

> The export-base approach is of most value when we interpret it loosely by stressing the importance of changing national demand patterns in regional growth and the dependence of a region's growth rate upon the growth performance of the national economy.

Quite often, local officials take a rather parochial view of the development process and concentrate their efforts on attracting industry away from other areas rather than on improving factor productivity, expanding social overhead capital, or engaging in other activities that might be somewhat more fundamental. To be sure, if promotional activities are successful in attracting a new manufacturing plant, the region will almost undoubtedly grow. The addition of, say, 200 new jobs in the plant may ultimately lead to the creation of 300 or 400 additional jobs in the region. There will definitely be a multiplier effect.[c] If some industries are attracted to an area because of the existence of certain water resources, then investments in those resources to expand or improve the quality of services flowing therefrom may cause industry location in the region. Regional economic growth could be expected to follow in the way predicted by the export-base model.

Furthermore, population may be attracted to a region because of the availability of water resources, especially for recreation purposes. As studies of the industrial location process have indicated that labor supply availability is a primary locational determinant, such population movement might be followed by the location of new production units in the region. The extent to which water resource availability and cost is important in the industrial location decision is not clear, nor is the relationship between water and migration

---

[c]From a national point of view, however, this promotional effort may be regarded as wasteful because the plant would have been located somewhere and, thus, the effect on the national economy may have been approximately the same.

decisions. The nature of such decisions and the possible role played by water resources is discussed in Chapter 6.

A Supply Oriented Model of Economic Growth

The neoclassical model of economic growth provides an excellent tool for analyzing the growth impacts of an investment such as water development. Following the framework and much of the terminology of Meade,[5] consider an economic system where only one utility-producing product (Y) is produced. (This restrictive assumption will be relaxed later.) Three productive factors are employed, capital (K), labor (N), and resources from the natural environment (L) (including land, air, minerals, and water). Investment in water development may be viewed as the production of a capital good that combines with services of the natural environment (including water) and labor.

The production function can be thus described as $Y = f(K, N, L, T)$, where T stands for time and thus dates the period of production. T might thus be a proxy for a given "state of the art," and may change from one period of time to another. The output of product Y depends upon the quantities of the inputs available for use in the productive process in time period T and the level of technological advance being employed in period T.

Each of the factors is assumed to contribute to output. The respective marginal products for capital, labor, and the natural environment are

$$\frac{\partial Y}{\partial K}, \ \frac{\partial Y}{\partial N}, \text{ and } \frac{\partial Y}{\partial L},$$

respectively.

Any growth in output between two time periods, say T_0 and T_1, can be expressed in terms of the contributions of the various factors, including technical advance. Thus,

$$\Delta Y = \frac{\partial Y}{\partial K} \Delta K + \frac{\partial Y}{\partial N} \Delta N + \frac{\partial Y}{\partial L} \Delta L + \Delta Y' \qquad (3\text{-}16)$$

where $\Delta Y'$ is the increase in output due solely to technical advance.

Equation (3-16) can be rewritten as follows:

$$\frac{\Delta Y}{Y} = \frac{K}{Y} \frac{\partial Y}{\partial K} \frac{\Delta K}{K} + \frac{N}{Y} \frac{\partial Y}{\partial N} \frac{\Delta N}{N} + \frac{L}{Y} \frac{\partial Y}{\partial L} \frac{\Delta L}{L} + \frac{\Delta Y'}{Y} \qquad (3\text{-}17)$$

or

$$y = \alpha k + \beta n + \epsilon l + t \qquad (3\text{-}18)$$

where

$$Y = \frac{\Delta Y}{Y} \ , \ k = \frac{\Delta K}{K} \ , \ n = \frac{\Delta N}{N} \ , \ l = \frac{\Delta L}{L} \ , \text{ and } t = \frac{\Delta Y'}{Y} \ ,$$

and $\propto, \beta$, and ϵ are respectively the elasticities of production (e.g., $\propto = \partial Y/\partial K$ $\cdot K/Y$) of the factors capital, labor, and natural environment. Roughly, these elasticities represent the percentage changes in output that result from a one percent change in the inputs, given that the supplies of the other inputs and technical advance are unchanged.

Under the assumption of perfectly competitive product and factor markets and constant returns to scale, $\propto + \beta + \epsilon = 1$, and it can easily be shown that $\propto$, β, and ϵ represent respectively the proportion of output Y which would be paid out to each of the factors of production as a reward for its contribution to output. Thus, the distribution of income that results from any increased input utilization is determined.

If an investment in water resource development is undertaken, the initial impact on Y will be $\propto k$. But this is not all. At least two other types of adjustments will occur over time that will shift the level of output. Due to the increase in the supply of K, factor markets will adjust to new equilibrium positions and in the process Y will be affected; and the increase in K may cause shifts in the production function due to technical advance.

The first point results from the operation of the law of variable proportions. In equilibrium each of the factors is utilized up to the point where its marginal factor cost is equal to its marginal revenue product. In competitive factor markets the marginal factor cost equals the price of the factors. In competitive product markets the marginal revenue product of each factor equals its marginal physical product times the product price. The marginal physical product of the factor is assumed to be a decreasing function of the quantity of the factor employed relative to the quantities of the other factor employed with it. Symbolically,

$$\frac{\partial Y}{\partial K} = g \left[\frac{K}{L + N} \right] \ , \ \frac{\partial Y}{\partial L} = h \left[\frac{L}{K + N} \right] \ , \text{ and } \frac{\partial Y}{\partial N} = j \left[\frac{N}{K + L} \right] \qquad (3\text{-}19)$$

Thus, other things being equal, if K is increased, $\partial Y/\partial K$ would be expected to decline, and $\partial Y/\partial L$ and $\partial Y/\partial N$ would be expected to increase. The values of marginal product for resources from the natural environment and labor might be expected to exceed their prices, and these factor markets would be out of equilibrium. More of these factors would be employed until their marginal physical products declined to those levels required for a new equilibrium position, where the price of the factors equaled their respective values of marginal product. The reverse would hold for capital. Secondary effects on factor employment required for the reestablishment of equilibrium, therefore, must be inserted into Equation (3-16) in order to estimate the full impact on Y from the initial expenditure ΔK.

It was assumed in the formulation of Equation (3-16) that technical advance is purely output expanding and autonomous, i.e., introduced from sources outside the system. Thus its influence on output is expressed as $\Delta Y'$. In reality, technical advance may take quite a different form. It may not influence output at all, but may increase the efficiency of the factors, so that the same amount of product can be produced with smaller commitments of inputs. Technical advance may thus be natural resource saving, labor saving, or capital saving. In fact, for every given set of factor availabilities and factor prices, there is, in principle, an optimum technology which maximizes the productivity of all inputs. If the set changes, the optimum technology may change. Thus, when the productive system changes, as would be the case with most water development projects, the optimum technology would be altered. The output-expanding and/or resource-saving effects of these changes must also be assessed before the complete impact on output growth can be determined.

So far the regional production function has been limited to a single product and has been assumed to be closed. These restrictive assumptions will now be relaxed in order to consider allowance for multiple products that include those which produce disutility as well as utility, and opening the system to permit exports and imports.

Most types of water development are multipurpose; e.g., a dam is constructed that provides water for power generation, irrigation, and recreation. Using our former notation, these could be expressed as Y_1, Y_2, and Y_3, summarized as the Y_i. A concomitant of the production of these products may be the destruction of certain properties of a free-flowing river that has been dammed up; e.g., a stream fishery or a scenic canyon. These negative products of development are the Y_j. As a simple tallying device, suppose gross product (V) is defined as the difference between the positive contribution (Y_i) to welfare and the negative contribution (Y_j). Thus,

$$\Delta V = \Delta(Y_1 + Y_2 + \ldots + Y_n - Y_{n+1} - Y_{n+2} - \ldots - Y_{n+m}) \qquad (3\text{-}20)$$

Following the procedure used in Equation (3-16), ΔV can be expressed as follows:

$$\Delta V = \frac{\partial V}{\partial K}\,\Delta K + \frac{\partial V}{\partial N}\,\Delta N + \frac{\partial V}{\partial L}\,\Delta L + \Delta V' \qquad (3\text{-}21)$$

This formulation allows accounting for situations where investment changes the mix of products and includes unfavorable outputs as well as favorable ones.

To complete the analytical system, one further modification of the effects of investment in a given project will be considered. In addition to the final consumption goods that constitute part of the output of a productive process, intermediate goods in the form of productive factors that will be employed thereafter in the production of final goods may be produced. Actually, an investment may result either in an increment to the basic stock of productive factors or a decrement. For example, construction of a dam may increase the land area utilized in agricultural production by extending irrigation, or decrease it if the inundated area exceeds new land brought under production. Alternatively, the productive quality of the factors may be increased or decreased as a result of the project; irrigated land may be more or less productive than dry land, depending on moisture, fertility, drainage, and alkalinity conditions. These qualitative changes in the factors, as well as the quantitative ones, must be evaluated.

Let $\Delta\hat{K}_i$, $\Delta\hat{N}_i$, and $\Delta\hat{L}_i$ represent the p favorable changes in both the quantity and quality of capital, labor, and natural environment inputs, respectively, and $\Delta\hat{K}_j$, $\Delta\hat{N}_j$, and $\Delta\hat{L}_j$ represent the q unfavorable changes in the same inputs. Then,

$$\Delta V' = \sum_{i=1}^{n} \Delta Y_i - \sum_{j=n+1}^{m} \Delta Y_j + \sum_{i=1}^{p} \Delta\hat{K}_i + \sum_{i=1}^{p} \Delta\hat{N}_i + \sum_{i=1}^{p} \Delta\hat{L}_i$$

$$- \sum_{j=1}^{q} \Delta\hat{K}_j - \sum_{j=1}^{q} \Delta\hat{N}_j - \sum_{j=1}^{q} \Delta\hat{L}_j \qquad (3\text{-}22)$$

The most general statement of the total impact of a change in any of the productive factors is the following:

$$\Delta V' = \frac{\partial V'}{\partial K} \Delta K + \frac{\partial V'}{\partial N} \Delta N + \frac{\partial V'}{\partial L} \Delta L + \Delta V'' \qquad (3\text{-}23)$$

Equation (3-23) could be rewritten in a manner exactly analagous to Equation (3-16) to yield an expression similar to Equation (3-17), and from there to an expression containing the elasticities of production of the factors in terms of the impact on the total system of proportional changes in the factors.

Now, permit the region to trade with other regions. In a closed regional system, of course, the utility of the residents of the region will be functionally related to V' to the extent that changes in the quantity and quality of the productive factors can be converted into final consumption commodities Y_i and Y_j. This will not hold, of course, in an open system where trade occurs. The extent of the improvement in utility that accrues to an open system depends on the terms of trade of the region in question with the outside world. If a region has great relative advantage in the production of certain commodities and can trade these commodities to other regions at favorable terms, the gains in utility of the open system over the closed one will be large. In addition, not only may the Y_i to be traded, but it is well known that some regions also export the Y_j (or the K_j, N_j, and L_j) in the form of polluted air and water or unemployment. The terms of trade must be very attractive to the exporting regions if these "disbenefits" can be exported at near zero prices.

The use of the neoclassical model in a regional context as described in this section has been criticized because of the assumptions of continuous full employment and perfect competition. The latter, although somewhat unrealistic, may not be overly restrictive; it is not clear that the implications of the model would differ significantly if other market structures were assumed. The full employment assumption does, however, pose problems because interregional differences in resource utilization are not only an empirical fact, but are one of the main foci of regional analysis. Offsetting these criticisms is the fact that the complete model gives explicit consideration to factor returns, intensity, and mobility—all of which are extremely important in regional growth analysis. The model is more realistic than the export-base concept in that it recognizes three sources of economic growth: capital accumulation; increased labor supply; and technical progress, as included in the following regional model.

A regional variant of the neoclassical model can be developed which makes explicit these sources of growth as well as taking into account interregional considerations.[6] Alter the production function so that labor, capital, and technical progress (T) are the relevant inputs and assume that all are functions of time. Then, from the production function for region i (it is assumed that each region produces a homogeneous output under identical production functions),

$$Y_i = f(K, N, T), i = 1, \ldots, m \tag{3-24}$$

the following growth equation can be derived:

$$y_i = a_i k_i + (1 - a_i) n_i + \rho_i \tag{3-25}$$

where y, k, n, and ρ are the growth rates of the four relevant variables (e.g., $y = (dY/dt)/Y$), and a and $(1 - a)$ are the shares of income accruing to labor and capital.[d]

As the model requires full employment growth, the rate of interest can serve as a mechanism to equal full employment savings with investment. The marginal product of capital must equal the interest rate (r) in equilibrium.

$$MP_k = a(Y/K) = r \tag{3-26}$$[e]

---

[d]Under the assumption of perfect competition, each factor is paid its marginal product, and, since the production function exhibits constant returns to scale, total output is exhausted by factor payments, thus $a = (dY/dK) \cdot (K/Y)$ and $(1 - a) = (dY/dN) \cdot (N/Y)$

[e]Note that $[a \cdot (Y/K)] = (dY/dK) \cdot (K/Y) \cdot (Y/K) = dY/dK$

If r is given, Y and K must grow at the same rate if a is to be constant. Thus for steady state growth y_i must equal k_i. Substituting y_i for k_i in (3-25) yields

$$y_i = \frac{\rho_i}{(1 - a_i)} + n_i \qquad\qquad (3\text{-}27)$$

and, for the system,

$$\frac{\rho_i}{(1 - a_i)} + n_i = \frac{\rho_i}{(1 - a_j)} + n_j; i, j = 1, \ldots, m \qquad (3\text{-}28)$$

Flexibility in the capital-labor ratio which causes changes in a_i is the key feature. Differences in rates of technical change and/or labor supply can be offset by varying factor intensity.

If factors flow freely across regional boundaries, factor returns and growth rates should converge. Regions with high capital-labor ratios will have a high marginal product of labor and low marginal product of capital. These regions should experience capital outflows and labor inflows. Opposite flows will be experienced in regions with low capital-labor ratios. This should result in convergence of rates of factor returns and growth rates of income among regions. However, reluctance to migrate, rapid natural increase, and/or a shift in marginal production functions may alter the conclusion of equilibrating interregional factor flows. The existence of economies of scale and agglomeration in high-wage urban industrial areas may offset the tendency for factor returns to converge. In this case, moreover, it is clear that the assumptions of identical production functions among regions is no longer valid.

Capital accumulation, an important source of growth in the model, would include private as well as social overhead capital, the latter including water-related capital items such as reservoirs, waterways, hydroelectric power plants, etc. The aggregative nature of the model does not allow identification of the differential effects on regional output of changes in specific types of capital. For example, the economic impact of an investment in a new highway relative to a similar expenditure on an irrigation project is a most relevant comparison, but one that this model is not capable of making. It might be possible to disaggregate the variables in the model to take account of the impact differences, as between private and social capital accumulation, and also the differential growth effects of investment in the several classes of capital goods within each of these broad categories.

Probably the most important feature of the model is its emphasis on supply factors in contrast to the export-base models which are demand oriented. Certainly long-run growth is heavily dependent on growth in supplies of labor and capital inputs. Furthermore, growth in output per capita generally requires technological progress or increases in the amounts of capital used per unit of labor.[f] Under the right conditions, a water-resource investment in a region should raise the capital-labor ratio sufficiently to increase output and, therefore, income per capita.

If maintenance of aggregate demand sufficient to bring about full employment is largely a national policy goal, then perhaps regional analysis should focus on the supply side, not only in terms of resource quantity but also quality and location. Under such conditions the appropriate framework for analyzing regional growth would be a supply-oriented model such as the one just outlined.

Borts and Stein [7] used the neoclassical growth framework in their comprehensive investigation of interstate differentials in economic growth. Myrdal [8] hypothesized that there is an inherent tendency for free market forces to perpetuate regional differences in growth rates. Growing areas will experience capital shortages and will import needed capital from the under-developed regions, causing a further widening of the growth differential. Borts and Stein accept the premise that the growing region will tend to be a new importer of capital, but show that regions with below average incomes are likely to have above average growth rates, and that there is a tendency for growth rates and per capita income levels to converge.

Using the continental United States as a sample of 48 regions, it was shown that growth in manufacturing employment depends significantly on the ratio of manufacturing to total employment, and the rate of in-migration to the region. Neither the prevailing wage rate nor the region's industrial structure was significant in explaining differential growth rates among regions. Those regions that had experienced a secular reduction in the rate of employment growth (i.e., evidence of a sort of economic maturity), were found to have largely exhausted gains from intersectoral shifts of labor, and experienced a decline in the rate of growth of labor supply, due to the inverse relationship between urbanization and net reproduction rates.

The concept of intersectoral allocative efficiency has important implications for water resource development, to the extent that such investments may change the rate at which factors are moving from low to high productivity employment. The idea can be formalized in the following way. Assume there are P industries in the region, each producing under a production function yielding constant returns to scale. If they operate in a perfectly competitive market structure, each factor will be paid its marginal product and factor payments will exhaust output. Let r_i and w_i denote the marginal products of capital and labor respectively. Then, for region i,

$$Y_i = r_i K_i + w_i N_i \qquad\qquad (3\text{-}29)$$

[f]Per capita output can also be expanded by reducing the level of unemployed resources and/or by the elimination of resource misallocation. The latter is defined as shifting productive factors to employment where the marginal product is greater than is previous employment.

Maximum output requires that the respective marginal products be equalized among industries; that is $r_i = r$ and $w_i = w$ for all i, such that

$$Y = r K + w N \qquad (3\text{-}30)$$

where Y, N, and K indicate regional aggregates. In disequilibrium, where the average of the marginal products r' and w' is less than r and w we have

$$Y' = r' K + w' N < Y = r K + w N \qquad (3\text{-}31)$$

Rewriting (3-31) as

$$Y' = r K + w N + [(r' - r) K + (w' - w) N] \qquad (3\text{-}32)$$

the bracketed term is the economic loss due to inefficient allocation of factors among industries. In addition to gains from within region factor movements there are also potential gains from interregional factor movements, both within and among industries.

Both Denison [9] and Massell [10] have emphasized the importance of intersectoral factor shifts. Massell, in a major study, estimated that one-third of so-called technical change is really due to a more efficient allocation of productive factors among sectors. Denison, contrasting sources of economic growth in the United States and Europe, estimated that seven percent of the total increase in U.S. output between 1950-1962 was due to better resource allocation. He points out, however, that failure to maximize income does not imply failure to maximize welfare. Both workers and entrepreneurs may have objectives other than income or profit maximization. In addition to a degree of factor immobility, institutional obstacles imposed by government, labor organizations, and business may preclude maximum efficiency.

The Borts-Stein research supports the neoclassical concept that growth, at least at the regional level, is largely determined on the supply side by increases in factor supply and their productivity. They found that a powerful explanatory variable for employment change was prior change in labor supply schedules. Of particular importance in this regard is the increased labor supply made available to manufacturing by outmigration from the agricultural sector.[g] Therefore, in assessing the impacts of water-related investment on the regional

---

[g]While the sectoral "theory" of regional growth is more of a historical accounting of developmental stages than a true growth model, it is useful in explaining the release of labor from agriculture. Assume the following trends or conditions: a general rise in per capita income, a low-income elasticity of demand for agricultural products relative to manufactured goods, and a high rate of productivity increase in agriculture relative to manufacturing. Tendencies for prices and factor returns to show relative increases in the manufacturing sector imply shifts of both labor and capital from agriculture to manufacturing, assuming factor mobility.

economy, it is imperative that the extent of resource misallocation be known and the likely effects of such investments on changes in intersectoral allocation be predictable. The analysis must focus not only on such shifts within the project region, but must also include factor movements into and from the region, and, more specifically, the sectoral source and destination of these factors.

In the U.S. the movement of labor from agriculture into other sectors, particularly manufacturing, provides the best example of the elimination of resource misallocation. If the availability of low-cost water and/or hydro-power is a significant factor in attracting industry, then investment in those types of water resources should accelerate the agricultural-industrial shift of labor. An investment to provide irrigation water, to the extent it raises the return to farm operators and workers, should slow the outmigration from the agriculture sector. Of course, if the marginal productivity of labor in agriculture was increased by the availability of irrigation water, the differential between returns in agriculture and nonagricultural occupations would have been reduced, thereby reducing the magnitude of the misallocation.

Industry Structure Approach to Regional Growth

The work of Ashby [11] and Perloff, et. al.[12] has been instrumental in the development of an operational model for evaluating industrial structure and its relationship to regional growth. The analysis of growth by focusing on regional industrial structure and changes therein tends to be more directly applicable in empirical analyses than are the theories previously described. Since it considers industry structure in detail, however, it might be of more value at the operational level of regional analysis. In its simplest form this concept predicts growth based on the region's weighted representation of national industries. A region in which employment is concentrated in those industries which are growing rapidly at the national level should be expected to experience above average growth, while a region with a large proportion of lagging industries will tend to grow slowly, if at all.

Given a projection of national employment in industry i ($\hat{N}_{i.}$), employment in this industry for region j, ($\hat{N}_{ij}$), is predicted by

$$\hat{N}_{ij} = (\hat{N}_{i.}/N_{i.})\, N_{ij} \, *$$

(3-33)

---

*Note that

$$N_{i.} = \sum_{j} N_{ij}$$

That is, national employment is equal to the sum of regional employment. The circumflex is used to designate a projected year in projections appliacation or the terminal year in the analysis of an historic period. For Equation (3–34) note that

$$N_{..} = \sum_{i} \sum_{j} E_{ij}$$

That is, national employment is the sum of employment in all industries and regions.

However, empirical evidence suggests that this is a poor predictive tool. Regional industries do not tend to grow at the same rate as their national counterparts. Equally as important as industry mix is "input-output access," a term relating to proximity to input sources and final markets and the relative attraction of both (i.e., cost and quality of inputs, size and growth of markets, etc.).

The generalized industry structure concepts include both industry mix and relative "input-output access." It views regional employment change as being composed of three elements: (1) general trends in the national economy (the national growth effect); (2) the region's industry structure (the industry mix effect); and (3) the region's input-output access (the competitive effect). The national growth effect (N_j^n), the change in regional employment expected if employment in each regional industry grew at the overall average for the nation, can be written

$$N_j^n = \sum_i [(\hat{N}_{..}/N_{..}) - 1]\ N_{ij} \tag{3-34}$$

The industry mix effect, (N_j^i), the expected change in employment if each industry in the region grew at the national rate for that industry, is given by

$$N_j^m = \sum_i [(\hat{N}_{i.}/N_{i.}) - (\hat{N}_{..}/N_{..})]\ N_{ij} \tag{3-35}$$

and the competitive effect, (N_j^c), by

$$N_j^c = \sum_i [(\hat{N}_{ij}/N_{ij}) - (\hat{N}_{i.}/N_{i.})]\ N_{ij} \tag{3-36}$$

which measures the change in regional employment holding industry mix and national growth constant, i.e., a measure of regions' relative input-output access.

Although, strictly speaking, this is not a regional growth model, it does provide an orderly way to analyze the previous employment growth experience of a region or one or more regions. It is best thought of as an accounting scheme for classifying sources of employment growth.[h]

Perhaps the key feature of this approach is the recognition that regional growth is highly dependent on forces existent in the national economy (as

---

[h]The value of shift or input-output access analysis either as an analytical or predictive tool has not been empirically demonstrated. Based on manufacturing employment changes in 14 SMSAs, Brown [13] argues that the model is a poor predictor of future changes–in fact, it is grossly inferior to one that merely projects employment in each regional industry at that industry's historic national growth rate. Even more damaging is the evidence that suggests that the competitive element is a random variable. The value of the competitive element in one five-year period appears to be independent of the value in the next five-year period. It is difficult to imagine that fundamental input-output access factors are changing that rapidly. It should be emphasized, however, that Brown's results are based on a small sample of areas, and should be regarded as tentative.

measured by the national growth and industry mix shifts), but that the impacts of these forces can be tempered by the differential input-output access among regions. Empirical research has demonstrated that an industrial mix weighted in favor of rapid growth industries is no guarantee of above average regional growth, nor does unfavorable industry mix imply slow growth. Because of superior transportation systems, labor force quality, or closer proximity to developing markets, a region in the latter category can exhibit a high rate of growth.

Among some state and regional economic or industrial development agencies there appears to be acceptance of the main facets of the industrial structure approach. A large part of their activities amounts to little more than advertising and promotion designed to attract new plants to the area, particularly those in rapidly growing industries. Strong aspects of the state's relative input-output access—such as low labor costs, proximity to national markets, etc.—are emphasized. In some cases, financial inducements in the form of property tax exemptions or provision of land and/or buildings by a local authority are also offered, the objective being to convince businessmen that they have reduced the cost of operating at that location. Although most evidence indicates that financial incentives tend to have little or no effect on the macro (wide-area) industrial location decisions, their use has continued to increase, particularly among the low-income, nonindustrialized states.

Such development activity is useful to the extent it is successful in attracting capital into an area characterized by unemployment and reluctance to migrate. In such a situation it should result in both increased national and regional income, assuming the capital has not been withdrawn from productive use in another region. Such activity may lead to regional balance, and there is some evidence that there are complementarities in regional development such that a system of regions similar in income and industrial structure may be able to grow faster than a system of economically dissimilar regions.

For our purposes, the influence that water resource development has on a region's relative input-output access must be examined closely. On the surface it would appear that a region which can offer large quantities of good quality water at low prices, possibly together with low cost hydroelectric power, would have an advantage in attracting both human and physical capital. Under these circumstances the competitive shift, and changes therein over time, should be a useful variable for measuring the economic effects of various types of social investment.[i]

There are many other factors to consider, however, and it may be that water and related assets may be of secondary importance, and the net effect of investment in water resources might be difficult to estimate.

---

[i]Indeed, this measure was used by Howe [14] in what is probably the most widely referenced article on the role of water in regional growth.

Summary

The purpose of this chapter was to provide a brief review of the state of regional economic growth models as a means of establishing part of the background against which water resource investments could be evaluated. The export-base, neoclassical, and industrial models were presented as examples of the diversity of thinking about the growth process in a region. While none of these models offer a comprehensive view of that process, all of them contain features that are useful in explaining, predicting, and understanding the process. In each case, an attempt was made to appraise the way in which water investment would enter the model and its probable impact on economic growth. In general, it was found that the aggregative nature of these constructs allowed only qualitative and somewhat tentative conclusions to be drawn about such impacts.

Certain a priori expectations, such as the influence of water availability on the location of people and industry, and the movement of factors of production among sectors (e.g., the shift from agriculture to industrial employment), were hypothesized, and their potential role in economic growth examined. Definitive statements on these expectations must await a more detailed examination of roles played by the various water resources. This will be the major thrust of Chapters 4 and 5.

Notes

1. For a comprehensive review of the theory of economic growth, see: Edwin Burmeister and A. Rodney Dobell, *Mathematical Theories of Economic Growth* (New York: MacMillan, 1970).
   F.H. Hahn and R.C.O. Mathews, "The Theory of Economic Growth: A Survey," *Economic Journal*, LXXIV, 296 (December 1964) 779–902.
   Joseph E. Stiglitz and Hirofumi Uzawa, eds., *Readings in the Modern Theory of Economic Growth* (Cambridge, Mass.: The MIT Press, 1969).
   Regional economic growth models are reviewed in: George H. Borts and Jerome L. Stein, *Economic Growth in a Free Market* (New York: Columbia University Press, 1964).
   Hugh O. Nourse, *Regional Economics: A Study in the Economic Structure, Stability and Growth of Regions* (New York: McGraw-Hill, 1963).
   Harry W. Richardson, *Regional Economics: Location Theory, Urban Structure, Regional Change* (New York: Praeger Publishers, 1969).
2. The most complete statement on this theory is found in the series of articles by Richard B. Andrews, "Mechanics of the Urban Economic Base," *Land Economics*, XXIX–XXXI (1953–1956). These are reprinted in Ralph W. Pfouts, ed., *Techniques of Urban Economic Analysis* (Trenton: Chandler-Davis, 1960).
3. For a comprehensive treatment of this point, see: Richard F. Muth, "Differential Growth Among Large U.S. Cities," (working paper CWR15,

Institute for Urban and Regional Studies, St. Louis: Washington University, 1968).

4. Harry W. Richardson, *Elements of Regional Economics* (Baltimore: Penguin Books, 1969), p. 54.

5. J.E. Meade, *A Neo-Classical Theory of Economic Growth* (London: Allen and Unwin, 1961).

6. This model is similar to that developed by Richardson, in *Regional Economics: Location Theory, Urban Structure, Regional Change*, pp. 331–336.

7. Borts and Stein, *Economic Growth in a Free Market*.

8. Gunnar Myrdal, *Economic Theory and Under-Developed Regions* (London: Duckworth, 1957).

9. E.F. Denison, *The Sources of Economic Growth in the United States and the Alternatives Before Us*, Supplementary Paper No. 13 (New York: Committee for Economic Development, 1962).

10. B.F. Massell, "A Disaggregated View of Technical Change," *Journal of Political Economy*, LXIII, (1961) 547–557.

11. Lowell D. Ashby, "Regional Change in a National Setting," (Staff working paper No. 7 in economics and statistics, U.S. Department of Commerce, 1964).

12. Harvey S. Perloff, et al., *Regions, Resources and Economic Growth* (Baltimore: Johns Hopkins Press, 1960).

13. James Brown, "Shift and Share Projections of Regional Economic Growth," *Journal of Regional Science*, IX, 1 (April, 1968) 1–17.

14. Charles W. Howe, "Water and Regional Economic Growth in the United States, 1950–1960," *Southern Economic Journal*, XXXIV, 4 (April, 1968) 477–499.

4

Welfare, Preferences, and Measurement of Growth

In this chapter, regional development concepts are taken from the previous considerations of regional delineation and models of growth and applied to particular indicators of growth. Accounting and measurement of consumer utility, productivity and allocation of factors, interregional effects, and a critique of current national income measurement procedures are utilized to provide a basis for a review of a regional accounts system. This system would include the stock of capital, including water resources, and allow measurement of the effects following changes in these stocks.

Consumer Utility in Economic Growth

The analysis begins by postulating a utility function and considering the process of regional economic growth in a fundamental way. Such a framework will permit the delineation of broad categories of impacts of water resource development, and will provide insights into relevant growth-producing activities and the associated accounting and measurement problems.

Consider a closed regional economy. For a typical consumption unit such as a family, utility derived from consumption over some relevant time period can be described as follows:

$$U = U(Y_i, Y_j) \tag{4-1}$$

where the Y_i are final consumption goods produced in the region which provide utility $\partial U / \partial Y_i > 0$, and the Y_j are final consumption goods, also resulting from production processes, which produce disutility $\partial U / \partial Y_j < 0$. An example of Y_i would be the power generated by an internal combustion engine that permits people in an automobile to be transported to a desired destination. Using the same example, Y_j would be the pollutants which result from emissions of such engines and which enter the air, where they are consumed by human beings.

The utility function is expressed in this way because recent studies [1] have shown that practically all production processes simultaneously produce "goods" which contribute to utility (and thus to the standard of living), and "bads," in the form of waste residuals, which produce disutility and detract from the standard of living. Often these wastes are inflicted upon the common-property natural environment. Of course, the extent of the disutility created by these Y_j depends on preference functions of the consuming units and the assimilative capacity of the natural environment.

Since World War II, a growing economy has been one of the economic policy goals of most countries. Growth has also been one of the most prevalent and important goals of subnational governments. Nearly all states have their agencies of planning and development, and county and local governments have their chambers of commerce, all of which have economic growth at the very center of concern.

In recent years, this preoccupation with growth has been challenged. It is now widely believed that increased production resulting from economic growth produces undesirable as well as desirable consequences. This view was first articulated by E.J. Mishan,[2] who argued that our desires for bigger, better, and faster objects to satisfy insatiable appetites and whims have produced a social sickness termed "growthmania." Growth should be considered not as an end in itself, but only as a means of promoting well-being. Thus, the identification of economic growth as progress is hardly universally acceptable today. In fact, it is debatable whether or not it is acceptable to even a majority of the American people. The recent fate of the American SST is eloquent testimony that many people, including the majority of senators and congressmen, are aware that the costs as well as the benefits of at least certain types of growth must be carefully weighed.

It must be demonstrated, therefore, that increased economic activity will enhance the level of well-being of some human beings more than it diminishes the well-being of others. Our concepts and measures of growth, then, should be capable ultimately of reflecting at least some aspects of levels of human well-being. In the chapters that follow, these issues will be a primary concern as investment in water resource development is discussed.

Concepts of Welfare

Few would disagree with the presumption that the consumption of goods and services by human beings is an important, but not the only, contributor to human well-being. Some activities of mind and spirit also affect well-being and cannot be meaningfully described in a commodities framework. This caveat need not pose a problem, however, since the primary concern is the relationship between "economic" growth in the form of produced commodities and human well-being.

Commodities (goods and services) are converted into human satisfaction by the process of consumption. The level of satisfaction attained depends on the preference functions of the consumers and the commodities available to be consumed. The effective availability of commodities is related to three fundamental factors: the beneficence of nature and public institutions which provide "free" consumable commodities, i.e., there is no *quid pro quo* payment for commodities by the consumers; the effectiveness of the market in providing a wide variety of commodities at market-determined prices; and the purchasing power available to consumers in the form of wealth and income, which permits them to vote their preferences in the market.

It is obvious from the preceding paragraph that any indicator of well-being which focuses exclusively on the consumer's activity in the market may understate even that part of his total welfare accounted for by commodity consumption. Commodities produced by public agencies outside the market are not included. Perfectly rational people have been known to choose to live in areas where incomes are low and the market may not be extensive enough to provide the full range of goods and services, but where nature and/or public institutions are particularly generous in meeting their wants.

Furthermore, consumer purchasing power in the form of income and wealth will not guarantee the ability of the market to produce well-being. A given level of purchasing power will lead to more satisfaction if many, rather than few, market options are available to consumers, given the level of market prices. Thus, an expansion of the market will normally result in an expansion of choice by the consumer, and will raise the level of satisfaction. The market basket of commodities consumed can be quite different, much more diverse, and considerably more want-satisfying in a large sophisticated urban environment than might be the case in a remote rural one.

Despite these problems, per capita income, corrected for price level differences, is the most popular single indicator of human well-being. For most purposes, however, it is well to keep in mind that income, and wealth converted into income equivalents, is an accurate relative indicator of the level of well-being only to the extent that it can be assumed that "free" commodities and the extent of the market are unimportant, or, if important, are proportionate to income for all consuming units. Although some geographic differences in availability and prices of market goods are apparent in a mass consumption society such as ours, most goods and services are available in a national market to most people at roughly comparable prices, especially through national chain stores and mail order houses. But this is not sufficient reason to uncritically accept per capita income as a proxy for well-being. Public policy is deliberately directed toward providing benefits from the natural environment and various public services to American citizens regardless of residence location and income level. The value of these services as a proportion of per capita income is greater for poor than for rich people. This means that, on the average, people with per capita incomes of $4,000 per year may not be ten times as well off as those with $400 per year. Thus, per capita income may well be a biased indicator of the level of well-being, with the well-being of low-income people being understated.

Another problem with using per capita income as a proxy variable for well-being hinges on the relationships among per capita income, welfare, and the age distribution of the population. The composition of the consumption bundle of goods and services chosen by the family is partially determined by the age of various family members. The needs and wants of children tend to be less costly in real income terms than those of adults. Thus, the average welfare of a family unit in a region with per capita income of $2,500 and a relatively high proportion of its population under age 17, would seem to be higher than the welfare of an average family in a region of the same per capita income with a low proportion of its population under age 17. The budget resources in the former case can be "stretched" to include more of the varied and sophisticated consumption items for the relatively smaller number of adults than in the latter case, where there is a high proportion of adults.

An alternative to per capita income that may be a better indicator of the level of well-being is family income. Family planning is widely practiced in the United States. Child bearing usually results from the deliberate choice of the parents to have additional children. If so, children can be considered to be a superior alternative to other competing uses of the family's income and wealth resources. Thus, it can be assumed that additional children enhance the welfare of the family unit. Almost inevitably, despite the subsidies which increase family size, such as the income tax exemption for dependent children, increasing the size of the family will reduce the per capita income of the family, so long as the children remain out of the work force, and perhaps even afterward. In having more children, therefore, people seem to be deliberately choosing an alternative which results in a reduction in per capita income, even though total family income may be little affected by increased family size. Family income may thus be a less-biased representation of the level of well-being than is per capita income.

Finally, a word should be said about the problem of inferring well-being from any objective indicator such as per capita income. Since well-being is a purely subjective concept, no known objective criterion has been found to measure and compare the well-being of two or more consuming units. At the margin, a dollar of income may have quite different utility to one consumption unit than to another, because of variation in the levels of income and wealth among families and differences in tastes and preferences. It is widely believed that the poor attach higher utility to marginal income than do rich people, but such a belief is impossible to prove. One of the tenets of scientific welfare economics is that it is simply invalid to make interpersonal comparisons of utility at all.

It is well to keep in mind these warnings about the use and interpretation of per capita income as a well-being proxy. Because of its popularity, however, and because no clearly superior alternative is available, it will be assumed in this study that any policy which increases per capita income will tend to increase the average level of human well-being.

Of course, per capita income may not always rise as regional income increases. In fact, per capita income may increase, decrease, or remain the same. Per capita income may rise because aggregate income increases faster than the region's population, or because population falls more rapidly than aggregate income falls. Increases in regional aggregate income may occur concomitantly with decreases in per capita income if population grows faster than income. Thus, it is important that the impact of public investments, such as water resource development, be described and assessed both in terms of total income, such as the net regional product described in a later section, and in terms of per capita income.

Levels and Distribution of Welfare

The most troublesome of all theoretical problems relating public investment to welfare are the relationships between welfare and economic efficiency and welfare and income distribution. It can be demonstrated that optimal resource allocation is achieved when three efficiency conditions are met by the economy. These are: an exchange optimum, which requires that the marginal rate of substitution of all goods consumed in the economy be the same for all persons consuming the goods in question; a production optimum, which requires that the marginal rate of transformation of all productive factors utilized by firms in the economy be the same in the production of all goods where such factors are employed; and a "top level" optimum, which builds on the preceding two, and requires that the community's marginal rates of substitution among consumed goods be equal to the community's marginal rates of transformation in production of goods produced.

In the absence of external effects, achieving these efficiency conditions results in a maximization of total income or community output. Given the population and/or the number of families in the region, average per capita or per family income is also maximized. So long as income distribution questions are ignored and per capita income is accepted as the indicator of welfare, meeting the efficiency conditions results in a maximization of social welfare.

These same principles of efficiency constitute the logical bases for so-called benefit-cost analysis. The approach is to determine whether or not investing in a specific project, such as a water resource development project, is consistent with a maximization of output and welfare for some relevant political unit, such as a nation or subnational region. The evaluation procedure requires that the scarce resources utilized by the project be evaluated at their "true" discounted social marginal opportunity cost, and that the benefits be evaluated at their "true" discounted social marginal values. If the benefits exceed the costs, the project passes the benefit-cost test, and construction of the project is required if economic efficiency is to be achieved and welfare is to be at a maximum.

If this process appears to be a simple task, a warning is well in order. Enormous difficulty is encountered in both principle and practice in the evaluation of costs and benefits and the selection of an interest rate for discounting purposes. Economists disagree over evaluation procedures. But even if the evaluation task can be achieved, considerable argument exists on what the evaluation means in terms of efficient utilization of resources and enhancement of welfare. Promulgators of the theory of "second best" have shown that if institutional or financial constraints of some kind prevent the achievement of an efficiency optimum everywhere in the economy simultaneously, there is no completely rigorous way of demonstrating that achievement of efficiency in the case of a single project will always move the total economy toward greater efficiency and welfare toward a maximum.[3] Notwithstanding the absence of proof, it is submitted that most economists accept the proposition that the greater the number of efficient sectors or projects, the greater will be the aggregate efficiency of the total system.

Fortunately, economists are not concerned only with the average level of per capita income in assessing the impact of a project on welfare. While it may be true that a given project increases average incomes, it will almost always be the case that some individual incomes will be increased in a given region and some will be decreased. The welfare of some people will thus be enhanced and that of others diminished. In this event, by what criterion can it be argued that community welfare has been increased (or decreased)?

The answer provided by the new welfare economics is that no unambiguous criterion exists that can reveal whether or not there has been an increase in total welfare. Individual gains and losses cannot be aggregated because no mechanism is available to make interpersonal comparisons of utility. Therefore, there is no way to aggregate individual utility functions into social or community utility functions. Thus, even if a project passes the benefit-cost test, aggregate welfare may be higher or lower, depending on how the gains and losses are distributed.

If some vehicle were available to redistribute incomes (say a pure income transfer program of some kind), then it might be possible to use income transfers to insure that there were no losers. If the project met the efficiency conditions as set forth above, and thus passed the benefit-cost test, the resources utilized in the project obviously would earn benefits that exceeded costs. In principle, therefore, if both the beneficiaries and the losers could be identified, the gainers could be taxed and the losers subsidized so that no one would be worse off because of the project. If the transfers are assumed to be costless, the conclusion is that any project which passes the benefit-cost test, together with a program of costless transfers compensating losers, would dominate any program of transfers in the absence of the project.[4] (An action A is said to dominate action B if all citizens are at least indifferent between A and B—that is, no one prefers B—and at least one person prefers A to B, i.e., A is said to be Pareto superior to B.) Thus, under these assumptions, the government should undertake all projects that meet the efficiency tests of benefit-cost analysis, and adjust "undesirable" income redistributions which result from the project by means of transfer programs.

Now consider the implications of dropping the assumption that pure income transfer programs are costless. In the real world they never will be completely costless for several reasons. Making the required transfer payments requires administrative costs. Identifying gainers and losers and determining the optimal income transfers to be made imposes heavy information costs, especially in the case of large multipurpose projects. A pure income transfer program may be morally unacceptable to at least some of the citizens, who would find it more palatable to receive subsidies on a *quid pro quo* basis in exchange for work, agricultural crops, etc. And, finally, the resources the government transfers must be raised by taxation, and no tax that is neutral on the allocation of resources is available.[5] Thus, we can safely argue that the transfer program itself will misallocate resources and thereby reduce the national income. The upshot is that any transfer costs required to redistribute income must be fully evaluated. Whether or not a public project should be constructed turns on whether or not the project benefits cover the project costs plus the income transfer costs.

Now, consider the other side of the coin. Suppose that the government wishes to utilize a public project to effectuate a more "desirable" distribution of income, i.e., to transfer income to certain poverty groups or to improve the relative income position of a lagging region. As a matter of fact, this seems to be the chief rationale of many public programs, even some water resources development projects.

If, in fact, "desirable" redistributions of welfare can be accomplished only by a given public investment project, there may be no alternative government action whatever which will dominate this project, even though it might fail the benefit-cost test. In comparing two projects, one which fails the benefit-cost test and one which passes it, no conclusion can be reached concerning the superiority of one over the other if the one which fails the test is the only means available to achieve "superior" redistributions of income and welfare.

Following Mishan,[6] these ideas can be illustrated graphically. Assume that commodity space is translated into utility space for a given community consisting of individuals A and B, and that a given collection of goods produced by the economy can be represented by Y_1. For example, Y_1 might be the particular collection of goods produced by the economy if a water resource project, which passes the benefit-cost test, is built. Suppose that the particular distribution of Y_1, which exists in the absence of any government transfer program, can be represented by Q_1 in Figure 4-1. On the axes of Figure 4-1, the utilities received by individuals A and B are represented. Q_1 is thus a given distribution of Y_1 between A and B.

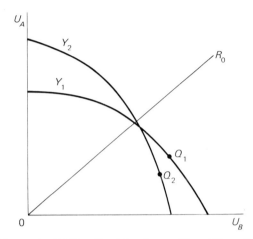

Figure 4-1. Alternative Utility Combinations without Hypothetical Transfers.

Now suppose all hypothetical distributions of welfare that might possibly be achieved through governmental transfers of Y_1 between A and B are plotted. These alternative distributions will form the utility possibility curve labeled Y_1 in Figure 4-1. All these points may or may not be politically feasible, depending on the acceptability and flexibility of the transfer program. This curve will be concave to the origin if the commonly accepted assumption of diminishing marginal utility is valid for A and B.

Suppose now that another collection of goods, Y_2, is produced by the economy. This may be the collection produced in the absence of the water resource project which helped produce Y_1. The utility possibility curve associated with Y_2 is so labeled in Figure 4-1.

Now assume that the community decides by some means that some distributions are better than others, that the best distribution of utility between A and B can be represented by ray OR_0 in Figure 4-1, and that distributions closer to OR_0 are better than distributions farther away.

These tools can now be used to make some judgments about Y_1 and Y_2 and their respective distributions. Suppose that Q_1 and Q_2 are the distributions of Y_1 and Y_2, respectively, in the absence of income transfer programs. Further, assume that no income transfers are permitted. Q_1 is Pareto superior to Q_2 because both parties are at higher utility levels. Q_1 also happens to be distributionally superior to Q_2, since it falls closer to OR. Therefore, Y_1 dominates Y_2, and is unambiguously superior by both efficiency and distribution criteria.

Consider next the utility possibility curves in Figure 4-2. Suppose that Q_3 is the only possible redistribution of Y_2 through transfers. Now, what can be

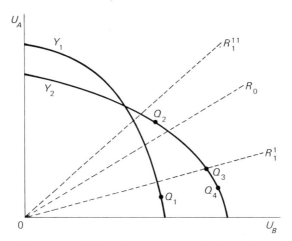

Figure 4-2. Alternative Utility Combinations with Hypothetical Transfers.

inferred about the relative superiority of Y_1 and Y_2? Q_2 is distributionally preferred to Q_3, which in turn is Pareto preferred to Q_1. Y_2 thus dominates Y_1 and must be preferred.

It could easily be shown that there could be a conflict between achievable distributions in Pareto preferredness and distribution preferredness. (Suppose Q_4, rather than Q_3, were the achievable redistribution of Y_2. Q_4 is Pareto superior to Q_1, but is distributionally inferior.) If so, there is no way of judging which collection and its achievable distributions would be preferred.

To return to the main argument, just as it was pointed out that no transfer program is likely to be costless, so also there are very few instances when public projects which fail efficiency tests are the only available means of achieving more desirable distributions of income and welfare. Contemporary American society has accepted (at least the majority of its legislators and jurists have accepted) a wide range of transfer programs: income tax exemptions, unemployment compensation, social security benefits, poverty and welfare programs, Medicare, and income programs in agriculture, to mention only a few. In fact, revenue sharing legislation has recently been enacted, and guaranteed annual incomes are on the horizon. Admittedly, these programs will not ensure that all losers from a given government project can be fully compensated for their losses. These programs do suggest, however, that specific government projects may not be the only acceptable ways of altering the distribution of welfare.

It is, of course, a difficult practical matter to know what constitutes better distributions of income and wealth. Individual opinions vary, because most people think that the distribution is better if their own position improves relative to that of others. Perhaps the most reliable indicators are guidelines set by national, state, and local legislators in statutes considered and passed; by the operating policies of governmental agencies; by the rulings of the courts; and by the Constitution, and its interpretation by the Supreme Court.

The unavoidable conclusion is that if a rigorous approach is taken to enhancement of welfare through investments in public projects such as water resources development, there is no escaping the necessity of making a complete analysis of both efficiency and equity impacts. If a project passes the economic efficiency test with a benefit-cost ratio exceeding unit, but has undesirable income distribution impacts, it should be demonstrated before it is approved that transfer programs are available and will be utilized to the extent necessary to offset maldistributions of income. The marginal costs of the transfer programs utilized must be added to project costs in the benefit-cost test. On the other hand, if a project is utilized to effectuate desirable income distribution objectives, but fails the economic efficiency test, it must be demonstrated before the project should be approved that alternative means of redistributing income are even more inefficient in a benefit-cost test.

Nothing as yet has been said relating the allocation of income over time to welfare. The question can be posed simply. Do fluctuations in family or per capita incomes from year to year cause welfare to be lower than a steady flow of income over time? The answer to this question depends upon whether families are risk takers or risk averters. If they are risk averters, they will attach some utility to stable incomes. How much utility will depend upon the degree of risk aversion.

The fact that people buy insurance even though the actuarial odds are not in their favor implies they are risk averters. Other people play poker or buy lottery tickets, which implies they are risk takers. Some people do both at the same time, which implies that they are risk averters when the cost of protection against a large income loss is small, and risk takers when the cost of the small chance to receive a large income gain is small. All this implies that people have a high aversion to being broke, but would take a certain small reduction in income for a small chance of becoming wealthy.

In any case, many public investment projects will alter the dispersion of the flow of net incomes over time in the project region. If some way could be found to evaluate the gain or loss in utility that results, it would be perfectly legitimate to impute this positive or negative value to the project as part of the benefit-cost test. We know of no scientific way this could be done; but the least that should be attempted is to point out the changes in the levels of income received over time as well as changes in the average level of income, so that the decision makers evaluating the project can consider them if they so desire.

Measurement of Regional Growth

The material in the previous chapter on regional growth theory is useful as a framework for seeing the interrelationships between growth, as represented by changes in output, and changes in the contributing factors of production and technology. It conceptualizes growth but does not deal with its measurement. For this purpose, some system of accounts that provides indicators of growth is needed. It will be shown in this section that many indicators may be used, but that all are subject to certain limitations. Much depends on what questions are asked. For example, in answering questions such as how much infrastructure might be needed in highways, schools, hospitals, recreational facilities, etc., in a given region, the level of individual or family well-being is not so relevant as the total population and income of the regional economy. In addition to indicators of per capita well-being, there should be indicators that accurately reflect the aggregate economic and demographic activity of the region.

The national income accounts have been designed to provide indicators of aggregate output, or alternatively, on the other side of the accounts, aggregate income to factor owners. Some of these indicators are gross national product, net national product, national income, personal income, and personal disposable income. Suppose the equivalents of these indicators could be employed at the regional level. The question is, how well would they serve as measures of the level of local economic activity. The analysis begins with a critique of the national income concepts as they might be applied at the regional level.

As implied in the previous section, economic growth is an increase in the physical quantities of goods and services produced in the economy and used for consumption. But if we must have a single indicator which shows the growth which has occurred, the indicator must have a way of meaningfully aggregating physically unlike goods and services. The national income indicators accomplish this by converting physical units of output into dollar values by multiplying the physical units by market prices. The dollar values of output are thus comparable and additive. Each unit of output is weighted in the aggregate value product by its price.

For the purposes of estimating real per capita and aggregate growth, one question must be raised about this procedure. Do the market prices used as weights accurately reflect the contributions of the respective units of output to aggregate income in the face of increasing physical output? The answer seems to be that, if product and factor markets are perfectly competitive, they do. If the demand for the product is less than perfectly elastic, however, the additions to income produced by output expansion will be reflected by marginal revenue rather than by price.

The existence of interdependencies among consumers in consumption, among producers in production, and among producers and consumers (i.e., externalities), means that market prices will often be inadequate value indicators of products and factors. The solution to the problem of these externalities, much easier accomplished in principle than in practice, is to estimate the disparities between private market values and social values (which include the values of the externalities) and use these social values in evaluating income increments. If externalities are present in consumption of the product, the market demand price will not reflect the social value of the product as it is consumed. By the same token, if externalities are present in production of the product, the product supply price will not reflect the total social productivity of the factors of production. Externalities may be either positive or negative, and when they can be shown to exist and can be meaningfully quantified, valuation adjustments may be made to reflect their significance.

Despite the obvious problems with the valuation procedure discussed above, there is probably no way that unlike physical magnitudes can be compared and aggregated except by converting them into monetary values. An even more serious problem relates to the statistical coverage of the traditional national income indicators. What would be desirable is an indicator that captures all changes in the level of output. As a rule, the income accounts provide good coverage of those goods and services which pass through the market, but fail to include many of those which do not. If the proportion of those not included to those that are is constant, some simple adjustments could be made in the output data to arrive at total growth. The statistical coverage, however, becomes more comprehensive as the economic activity becomes more complex and the market expands into more and more areas of the economy. No acceptable method for estimating the degree of output understatement has yet been found.

A still different kind of issue arises because of the need to compare productivity estimates over time in order to assess the growth that has occurred. It has been explained how the evaluation procedure permits comparability and additivity of unlike goods and services. To be comparable in real terms, however, these aggregate income estimates must be deflated by some price level index. At the regional level, no price index, such as the wholesale and consumer indexes, covers all of the outputs which are valued, and thus the use of an index will bias estimates of physical productivity. The GNP price deflator was designed to deflate gross national product, but nothing equivalent exists for a regional economy. If the cost is not too great, a similar index might be developed for each region.

Having stated some of the limitations of using any value of output or income approach to measuring growth, it will be useful to discuss the merits of various alternatives that appear to be available for this purpose. Economists and others have recognized that a gross measure of productivity, such as the real gross national product, is not the best indicator of the aggregate size of the growing economy. The reason is that part of gross output is needed to simply maintain the stock of capital, which is part of the productive base of the economy. In the national income accounts, the category called gross investment is the total expenditure for new capital. But a substantial part of gross investment is simply replacement capital, called capital depreciation allowance in the income accounts. Gross product less capital depreciation allowance is net product. It could be argued that the change in real net product is the best indicator of growth. Thus, net national product is the appropriate indicator for the entire economy, and something equivalent in concept should be developed at the regional level. Of course, some of the other concepts in the national income accounts may have relevance at the regional level, just as they do for some purposes at the national level.

It is conceivable that a growth indicator that can show regional changes in the purchasing power of private individuals and families may be desired. For this purpose, the regional counterpart of personal disposable income at the national level would be required. To compute personal disposable income, all direct and indirect taxes and corporate earnings not paid out in dividends but retained as net corporate saving should be subtracted from regional net product. Added back in should be transfer payments and interest on government debt. Most regional businesses selling to the public will find this indicator of growth most useful for estimating demand for their products. Unfortunately, personal disposable income data are not easily obtainable. At the national level, data are available only on a quarterly basis; and on a subnational level, not at all.

The national government does publish monthly statistics on personal income. Like personal disposable income, personal income removes corporate saving from net national product, but includes all transfers from government back to persons. Personal income eliminates corporate income taxes and other payroll taxes. It is regarded as an excellent substitute for personal disposable income for estimating consumer demand. The most significant advantage of personal income is that the U.S. Department of Commerce publishes personal income data by states, regions, and metropolitan areas. Thus personal income data are likely to be more accessible at the regional level than the other national income items, and will be more heavily utilized for descriptive and analytical purposes.

The productivity accounting system is seriously incomplete. It has been suggested that the capital depreciation allowance represents the expenditures needed to maintain the productive capacity of the capital stock. But what about other factors of production? They have precise parallels to capital consumption resulting from the process of production. Labor also depreciates as production occurs, and maintenance of the stock of human capital (labor) at a certain base level requires investment in training, schooling, health, etc. Resources taken from the natural environment are depleted and to this extent should be netted out of gross productivity figures as is done in the depreciation of capital. This point is equally relevant with respect to factor quality as well as quantity. If the quality of the stock of human, capital, and natural resources declines over time, latent productivity of the economy has declined, and these deleterious changes should be subtracted from the net product of the system.[7] Alternatively, if quality of the factor stock improves due to technical advance and increases in knowledge, this improved latent capacity to produce should be added to the net product actually produced over a given time period.

As the accounting system does not directly reflect these changes, their importance can only be surmised from empirical studies. Denison,[8] Schultz,[9] Griliches,[10] and others have shown that much more than half of per capita productivity increases in the United States have resulted from improvement in the quality of the factors of production as represented in increased educational levels, more adequate knowledge, and increased quality of capital embodied in technical advance. While it is true that over time this improved factor quality results in output increases which are captured in the income accounts, the inherent growth in the productive capacity of the system between any two finite dates of time will be understated by including only output increases, if the future productive capacity of the inputs is increasing over the period in question.

Perhaps the greatest limitation of the productivity accounts is the manner in which they deal with negative final products. These are the final outputs of production which cause disutility to human beings, and which are generally thrust upon the common property natural environment in the form of waste residues and environmental despoliation. They also take the form of external diseconomies, such as urban crowding, congested traffic, and crime.

The measurement problem is easy to illustrate. Those economic activities that pollute our environment and congest our cities contribute positively in the growth accounts.[11] In fact, whatever private and public remedial action is taken to restore the environment is also added. The nonsense conclusion is that the faster we pollute the faster we grow, providing we attempt to invest in restoring what we first ruin. Thus, if the costs of economic growth were fully and accurately assessed, especially those negative products which hide from the income accounts, the growth performance of the industrial nations would not be nearly so impressive as national accounts indicate. It is even possible that many industrial regions which suffer large disbenefits of the kinds suggested here have grown at negative rates, even though population has increased and net product, as presently measured, shows healthy growth. It is clear that a more accurate set of national and regional accounts that will be more inclusive in showing product and factor disbenefits, as well as benefits, is needed.

Regional Accounts Systems for Measuring
Economic Growth

Having dealt with the conception and measurement of growth in the previous section, it will be useful to discuss systems for accounting for regional growth, especially as they relate to public investments, such as water resources development.

The traditional tools for measuring economic activity focus on current flows of income, saving, investment, etc. As such, they are somewhat incomplete, as they do not account for either change in, or the level of, the national or regional stock of reproducible capital. Furthermore, the crucial relationships between these flows and changes in the stock of capital, and between stocks and changes in flows have been somewhat neglected. This omission is largely explained by the purpose of existing accounting systems, which were designed to measure short-run changes in output and employment, particularly those associated with particular changes in federal government policies. Under such short-run concepts it is generally assumed that the capital stock, labor supply, and technical conditions of production are fixed, or, if variable, are of a second order of importance. On the other hand, the degree of utilization of existing resources, particularly labor, is of critical importance.

A comprehensive system of regional accounts should focus on the spatial distribution of national long-run economic growth, as well as on short-run cyclical change.[a] Those aspects of the national income accounting framework that are considered given are often variable in a regional accounting framework. The stock of capital (both public and private), including buildings and equipment and labor, are variables, both in terms of quantity and quality. Land, although strictly speaking not a reproducible resource, should be included in the capital stock, as its potential use and value changes with transportation innovations, general regional growth, and technological advance.

If the accounting system is to emphasize the spatial incidence of national economic growth, regional growth and change should be evaluated relative to a set of national efficiency and equity goals. Thus the regional and national accounts systems would be integrated, rather than being separate constructs, with the latter possibly being based on data provided by the former, assuming the regional delineation exhausted the nation's area.

Perloff and Leven, in one of the Committee on Regional Accounts' proceedings volumes,[b] envision a regional accounts system composed of the following accounts:[c]

1. *Current production and income account*, which would be essentially an interregional input-output matrix with rows outside the I-0 matrix tracing income flows to recipients. State and federal government activity would be included as an export component of the final demand vector.
2. *Nonhuman resources account*, which would include measurement of the stock of land, buildings, and equipment, both public and private. The

---

[a]Development of a fully integrated regional accounts system has suffered from the lack of a theoretically consistent and empirically sound theory of regional growth. It is probable that both will develop simultaneously, as elements of the accounts system are needed to test the theory, and the theoretical concepts are essential in the designing of the set of accounts.

[b]The committee was formed in 1958, and has been active since. Three published books, by Hochwald,[12] and Hirsch,[13] report the conference proceedings.

[c]Although each of the accounts contains useful information in and of itself, the key to the usefulness of the construct is the combining of all accounts into an integrated system whereby changes in one account can be traced directly to changes in the others.

latter category would be included at market value, while the former would
be measured in output capacity, as discussed below. Water resources, if
it could be demonstrated that they played an important role in regional
growth, would be included in this account.

3.   *Regional government account*, which would link local government revenues
     and expenditures to levels of economic activity in the region. An accounting
     for human and nonhuman resources, coupled with tax functions, would
     generate predictions concerning tax revenues, and the tendencies for these
     same resources to consume each kind of public service would yield informa-
     tion on the expenditures side.
4.   *Intraregional account*, which would record the spatial distribution of
     people and activity within the region. As such, it would be useful in trans-
     portation and land-use planning.

The measurement of the region's stock of human, reproducible nonhuman,
and nonreproducible resources is instrumental in measuring the potential output
levels of the region and in predicting the impacts of governmental policy
decisions. This suggests that an operational set of regional accounts would be
much more than a device for measuring past and current economic activity and
welfare. It would be a model through which the impacts of alternative policies
and/or investments could be predicted and compared. Regional growth theory
will play an important role in establishing the predicted stock impacts of a
given set of flows and the effect on economic flows occasioned by changes in the
region's capital stock. If stock-flow relationships were clearly defined and
quantitatively estimated, knowledge of a region's stock of capital, both human
and nonhuman, might be as valuable a measure of regional welfare as are the
flow data. For example, potential flows could be directly estimated from
measures of the capital stock. Furthermore, the range of producer and consumer
choice might be best estimated as a function of a broadly defined capital stock.

Accounting for the stock of socially-owned capital and assessing its impact
on regional growth (or decline) is important because that stock is subject to
direct policy control, unlike the private capital stock, where the quantity and
quality can be influenced only indirectly by public policy instruments. A
part of the public capital stock or social overhead capital is water oriented.
Examples would include dams, canals, reservoirs, and hydroelectric power
plants. The fact that a lake or river was originally endowed by nature to a region
makes it no less a part of the capital stock, in that improvements in quantity,
quality, and access are generally possible through public investment. The
inclusion of water-oriented capital in the regional accounting framework would
be subject to a demonstration that such capital has significant effects on
regional economic activity, and that such effects, if they exist, could be manipu-
lated and predicted with the degree of accuracy necessary for the use of water
resource investment as an economic policy tool.

Regional economic growth might be partially defined in terms of increasing the effective range of choice of residents of the regions both as consumers and producers. The use of the term "effective" suggests that income and profit flows (indicators of the ability to consume and produce) must coexist with stocks of consumption and production resources in order to attain "high" levels of regional welfare. A regional accounts framework for measuring regional activities would make a significant contribution toward making "effective range of choice" a measurable and operational concept.

In a region with "good" prospects for development, public policy will be directed toward those programs that will maximize the range of effective choice for resident producers and consumers, and, in the process, make the region an attractive locational alternative for immigrants and capital investment. Programs for regions with "poor" development prospects might best be directed toward easing the burdens of economic distress. These would include financial assistance for relocation and retraining, provision of information on employment opportunities in other areas, and direct welfare payments.

Measuring the range of effective choice would appear to be a nebulous, nonmeasurable concept, but this need not be the case. Range of choice is a function of both flow variables (income primarily) and a set of broadly-based resource stocks. Data on the flow variables are already available, although, as discussed above, there is probably some need for modification. Economists are just now beginning to seriously address the problem of resource measurement. For example, Leven, *et al.,* [14] devoted a significant part of their recent book in regional accounts to methods of valuing resource stocks. The ability to measure resource stocks will increase with increased realization of their importance in assessing growth rates and levels of welfare.

Levels of total and per capita income should be highly correlated with resource development, but there may be deviations because of decisions to consume more leisure time or where large investments are needed to repair environmental damage. The latter type of problem highlights the need to define income more comprehensively and/or to focus more on the quality and productivity of the regional resource set as an indicator of both growth and welfare. Also, by focusing on resource development, ambiguities in interpretation of economic trends should be reduced.

General, as opposed to partial regional growth would probably require balanced development of resources, both of the producer and consumer types (human resources are considered as a subset of the latter category). A region engaging in general resource development, that is, making investments that will increase the productivity of each resource, will be laying the groundwork for expansion of effective consumer and producer choice. A partial development effort, such as one concentrating on promotional schemes to attract new industry, may prove to be short-sighted, as a lack of broadly developed resources may repel potential "locators" and cause area residents to migrate to more developed areas, while firms may seek areas with highly skilled labor, efficient transport services, and developed land. In such an area, factor prices may be higher than in a poorly developed area, but per unit production costs lower because of the more productive resources.

Therefore, water resource development, in and of itself, should not be expected to be a panacea for regional development problems. Only if such development is part of a larger program of resource development, and if certain preconditions for growth exist, is it likely to be effective.

Resource development includes, but is not necessarily limited to, investment in the following: health facilities and programs; elementary, secondary, and higher education; vocational education; transportation systems; cultural resources; environmental resources; police and fire protection; and water resources. The dimensions of the environmental variable include "resource (air, water, etc.) purity," degree of congestion, crime rates, and visual or landscape characteristics such as orderly land use, quality and appearance of buildings and open spaces, etc.

Under this hypothesis, an additional measure of growth will be provided by the change in resource quality over time. Increased income, although likely to be colinear with quality improvement, will not be prima facie evidence of true economic growth. Accurate measures of such growth will require an entirely new set of regional accounts, in which quality must be explicitly included. Essentially, the argument is an assertion that the level of social welfare could be better estimated by measuring the availability and quality of a large set of resources, in combination with the more traditional flow measures, than by reference only to the latter. Furthermore, it is also important that regional growth be evaluated in terms of its contribution to a set of national goals—that is, regional growth, by definition, must be consistent with efficiency in resource use at the national level.

Hirsch, in an early article on regional accounts,[15] argues that regional analysts need to focus on measures that will estimate the "health and well-being" of a region. This concept of assessing regional welfare is not unlike the one just articulated. Hirsch begins by discarding the use of income data as a comprehensive welfare measure.

> Perhaps the most commonly used yardsticks for measuring the status of economy have been gross national product and national income. But are these two measures appropriate and, particularly, are they useful criteria for the determination of a region's health and well-being? The answer is an emphatic "No"! Instead, it appears promising to use a multiple set of criteria—i.e., the most significant properties by which the status of a region in two different time periods can be compared.[16]

Health and well-being is a function of consumption of goods originating in the private sector, the public sector, nature, nonprofit institutions, and the general environment. The dimensions of this measure include per capita personal real income; basic employment stability; net social benefits—a sort of consumer surplus in the public goods market, measured in terms of the difference between what people should be willing to pay for public goods and services and what actually is paid; economic growth—viewed not as an end, but as a means of providing superior opportunities (i.e., expanding the range of producer and/or consumer choice) for both residents and in-migrants; and amenities of life—measured in terms of the cost and availability of educational, recreational, and cultural programs, ease of inter- and intraregional transportation, and the quality of the living and working environment.

Notes

1. This relationship is clearly set forth by: Robert B. Ayres and Alan V. Kneese, "Production, Consumption, and Externalities," *American Economic Review*, LIV, 2 (June, 1967) 282–297.
    Kenneth E. Boulding, "The Economics of the Coming Spaceship Earth," in H. Jarrett, ed., *Environmental Quality in a Growing Economy* (Baltimore: Johns Hopkins Press, 1966) pp. 3–14.
2. E.J. Mishan, *The Costs of Economic Growth* (London: Staples Press, 1967).
3. See: R.G. Lipsey and Kelvin Lancaster, "The General Theory of Second Best," *Review of Economic Studies*, XXIV, 63 (October, 1956) 11–32.
4. See: D.F. Bradford, "Constraints on Public Action and Rules for Social Decision," *The American Economic Review* LX, 4 (September, 1970) 642–654.
5. See: Abba P. Lerner, "On Optimal Taxes with an Untaxable Sector," *The American Economic Review*, LX, 3 (June, 1970) 284–294.
6. E.J. Mishan, *Welfare Economics: An Assessment* (Amsterdam: North Holland Publishing Company, 1969).
7. See: Mishan, *The Costs of Economic Growth*.
8. Edward F. Denison, *The Sources of Economic Growth in the United States and the Alternatives Before Us*, supplementary paper No. 13 (New York: Committee for Economic Development, 1962).
9. T.W. Schultz, *The Economic Organization of Agriculture* (New York: McGraw-Hill, 1953).
10. Zvi Griliches, "The Sources of Measured Productivity Growth: United States Agriculture, 1940–1960," *Journal of Political Economy*, LXXI, 4 (August, 1963) 331–346.
11. B. Delworth Gardner, "Some Unresolved Issues in Measuring Economic Growth," Proceedings, Vol. 2, (Western Agricultural Economics Association, 1969) pp. 246–253.

12. Werner Hochwald, ed., *Design of Regional Accounts* (Baltimore: Johns Hopkins Press, 1961).

13. Werner Z. Hirsch, ed., *Elements of Regional Accounts* (Baltimore: Johns Hopkins Press, 1964).
    Werner Z. Hirsch, ed., *Regional Accounts for Policy Decisions* (Baltimore: Johns Hopkins Press, 1966).

14. Charles L. Leven, John B. Legler, and Perry Shapiro, *An Analytical Framework for Regional Development Policy* (Cambridge, Mass.: The MIT Press, 1970) p. 48.

15. Werner Z. Hirsch, "A General Structure for Regional Economics Analysis," in Hochwald, ed., *Design of Regional Accounts*, pp. 1–33.

16. *Ibid.*, p. 30.

Part II
Water in Regional Growth
and Development

In this major section, four chapters are devoted to considering the process by which water investment may influence the economic growth of a region. As regional economic growth is both socially desired and motivated, the latter in the sense that many government policies are designed to facilitate such growth, some attention should be devoted to water as a social resource, and an attempt should be made to estimate its social productivity, value, etc. But regional growth depends heavily on a set of decisions made in the private sector by firms and individuals as they react to regional differentials in resource availability and costs and to market potential, and explicit consideration must be given to the role of water resources in that decision-making process.

Leven has outlined three types of impacts associated with public investment projects: (1) "The impact on the economy extending from the resource utilization involved in the construction of projects." (construction impact); (2) "The availability to the population, either in increased quantities or at lower prices, of a variety of water or water-related services." (service impact); and (3) "A stimulation of economic development of the nation and its regions by way of the impact of various projects on the productivity and regional allocation of private, physical, and human capital." (development impact).[1] Clearly, interest should focus on the development impacts of a water project, but it should be kept in mind that it is the set of services provided by the project that influences the productivity and allocation of capital associated with development. Furthermore, as argued in the last part of Chapter 5, the construction and development impacts may not be independent for many large-scale projects.

In an a priori sense, water resource development, depending on the particular characteristics, might promote the growth of a region in one or more of the following ways. Resource scarcities which serve to constrain production levels would be alleviated. Under competitive conditions, relative increases in water input to the production function will tend to increase the marginal products and returns to other factors, including labor. And the introduction of water or more water might change the optimal techniques of production, thereby shifting upward the production functions, and thus increasing output per unit of input.

Consider some specific possibilities. Increased availability of water at reduced cost might be expected to improve the region's "input-output" access. Firms in the region should be able to increase their share of the market. This could be a positive force in attracting new industry and human capital into the region. Availability of water transportation would be expected to reduce average per unit transportation charges on some kinds of output and raw materials. This could have a significant and positive impact on total output and employment and on factor returns. Water-based recreation development would likely increase the welfare levels of many area residents, and might provide a base for the development of a tourist industry. The provision of irrigation water (or additional irrigation water) in many regions would allow more flexibility in crop selection, planting time, and production techniques, as well as generating increased output per acre.

Changes in economic activity as a result of water investment include direct and indirect effects. The former are defined as those changes in output, employment, and factor returns that are caused by firms, individuals, and governmental agencies reacting to a change in the availability and/or cost of services forthcoming from a water resource development project. While attention is concentrated on these direct effects, it must be realized that there will be a series of indirect changes in economic activity by way of forward and backward linkages from those activities directly affected. These indirect effects are very important, sometimes greater in magnitude than the direct impacts.

The analysis begins in Chapter 5 by discussing the nature of water resources, with special emphasis on the sources of water supply, the nature of water demand, the pricing system, and the interrelationships among the three. In some "water-short" areas, where it is alleged that inadequate supplies retard or place an upper bound on growth, the deterrent might be removed by viewing water in strictly economic terms, with emphasis on the use of more realistic pricing schemes to better allocate available water supplies among competing uses. In particular, the dichotomy characteristic of most price schedules for water, with one set of prices for agriculture and another for municipal-industrial users, is unrealistic and leads to a misallocation of the resource.

Chapter 5 begins by analyzing two ways in which water enters the productive process. In the first of these, water is considered as a direct input into the production function. Interest is focused on its influence on output and the marginal products of other inputs. In the other, emphasis is on the indirect role of water on production decisions.

Building on this work, the regional location decision of firms and individuals is analyzed with reference to the influence of water resources on this decision. Here the focus differs from that of the previous sections, in that an assessment is made of the efficacy of water resources in attracting capital, both human and nonhuman, from outside the regions. Previously, the concern was with the effect of water development on economic activity already taking place within the region. Consideration is given to the possibility that radical changes in water demands and supplies might change the severity of the water problem if, in fact, one actually exists. It is conceivable that changes in production techniques, in both agricultural and nonagricultural industries, will require far less water consumption per unit of output, and that improved waste treatment will significantly reduce the water consumption associated with pollution. Such developments would have the effect of increasing the effective supply of water (e.g., defined in terms of the amount of economic activity that could be supported by a volume of water). Practices such as ditch lining and phreatophyte control change the time, place, and type of use of water. Development of direct water-creating activities, such as desalinization and cloud-seeding, may also have significant influence on both the role of water investment in economic growth and the types of water-resource investments that should be made.

An outline of the sequence of developmental impacts on the regional economy following the construction of a large multiple-purpose project is presented in this chapter. The purpose of this discussion is to establish a "straw man" theory of developmental impacts that will serve as background for the analysis to follow. Economic growth and development in a region which could result from a major public investment project is described as a six-phase process. A final part of the chapter contains a discussion of possible interdependence between construction and development impacts of water investments within a regional context.

Chapter 7 presents a brief review of empirically-based research on the relationship between water availability and economic growth. Two points stand out in this review. Relatively little attention has been paid to the role of water in economic growth, and there is no consensus on the question of the importance of water in that growth process. In any event, this available research is of value in identifying certain relationships among key variables, and suggesting alternative methodologies for testing the water investment growth hypothesis.

The questions that are raised and addressed in this section include the following. Is water a necessary condition for regional growth? Is it a sufficient condition? Clearly, minimal amounts of water are a necessary condition for many activities, but are large supplies of good quality water sufficient to induce growth, and to what extent? What is the process or sequence of events by which water influences economic activity? What is the relationship between construction and developmental impacts? And, finally, are there technological possibilities on the horizon that might reduce or eliminate the "water problem"?

Notes

1. Charles L. Leven, "Some Problems in Establishing a National Water Policy," (statement before the National Water Commission, Washington, D.C., November, 1969) pp. 1–2.

5 Water: Its Characteristics and Future

Before probing deeply into the processes by which water services and development thereof can influence economic growth, some background is provided on the nature and characteristics of the resources in question. Consideration is given to the possibility that radical changes in production technology and/or consumer tastes might cause shifts in the demand and supply functions for water and related services. Such changes could have a significant effect on the type of water resource development program that would be suggested.

Nature and Characteristics of the Water Resource

The development of a region's resources is one approach to promoting the development of that region. Perloff and Wingo [1] have identified the characteristics of these resources that have the greatest development potential. They are strong demand for goods and services produced by using the resource, high comparative advantage for the region to produce these goods and services, low resource substitutability in the production of these goods and services, regionally strong forward and backward linkages in the production process, and high regional multipliers in terms of income and employment generation. In most respects, water is like other resources, and is subject to evaluation in the same way. It does have some unique characteristics, as do all other resources. These unique qualities will provide the subject matter for this chapter.

Because of problems of definition and measurement, and the institutional framework within which water and water-related services have been provided, the social value of water, and, therefore, the price that should be established, is difficult to estimate. Allegations that a region is suffering from a shortage of water often are based on noneconomic, and sometimes emotional, grounds that would not stand up under a more rational investigation based on sound economic principles. In many areas, so-called water shortages would disappear if a more efficient allocation of existing supplies was made. For example, claims that water for municipal and industrial use is in short supply in some parts of California are often used to support pleas for additional investment in water resource development. As more than 90 percent of water withdrawal in that state is for agricultural use, a significant part of that used in the production of low value crops, a transfer of water from agriculture to municipal uses is a very real and possibly less-costly alternative, although one that is usually given little consideration.

In some cases "water shortages" could be alleviated almost immediately by merely raising the price of water. In some parts of the country, not necessarily those characterized by large reserves of the resource, water is provided at such a low price per unit that it is considered to be essentially a free good, and little care is taken by users to insure that the water is managed carefully. Generally, the price of water is set by administrative decree or determined by the need to amortize part or all of the cost of a related investment. As little attention is paid to the more fundamental forces of supply and demand, these prices would approach a market determined price only randomly. A deviation between the actual price charged and the price that would be determined by market forces implies a misallocation of resources. Howe and Easter's summary [2] of the pricing policy of the Bureau of Reclamation is indicative of the nonmarket pricing methods employed:

> Costs allocated to power and municipal-industrial uses plus interest are to be paid back from user charges; irrigation costs are adjusted to a measure of ability to pay for water over a fifty-year period without interest and are further subsidized by excess power revenues; and costs allocated to flood control, navigation, salinity repulsion, and fish and wildlife activities are not considered reimbursable.

This dichotomy of the pricing system with one set of prices for agricultural users and another set for municipal and industrial users can only be justified on equity grounds—it is not consistent with maximum efficiency. As viewed from the public agency, however, price discrimination may well be justified, if the goal is to maximize revenue from water sales, and if the elasticities of demand among the various users are propitious. From the vantage point of this book, water pricing and allocation will be viewed in much broader terms than a government administrative agency would use.

As suggested above, the administrative determination of water prices, without regard to the market, makes it difficult to accurately identify water shortage or water surplus areas, since excess demand or supply is defined as a function of existing prices. An alleged water shortage might quickly disappear under a different pricing scheme. For example, the quantity of water demanded by agriculture under typical reclamation projects for low value forage crops, would probably decrease substantially if farmers were forced to pay the full cost of providing that irrigation water. In an area where limited water imposed a constraint on further output expansion, regional income might be increased by transferring water from low value uses, primarily agricultural, to higher value industrial and/or municipal uses. Such a resource reallocation would probably result from the establishment of one price to all users so that an industry, if it so desired, could bid away a significant share of water now being withdrawn by users where the resource productivity is lower. The critical economic variable here, of course, is the elasticity of demand by industrial users. Such transfers would increase income only if water was truly a constraint on production or, equivalently, if the water demand function is less than perfectly inelastic. This may be the case, as other factors, such as market or plant size and labor supply, usually appear to be limiting factors. In any event, so-called water shortages might better be resolved by more efficient use of existing supplies than by investing to create additional water supply.[a]

The assertion that income could be increased by intersectoral water transfers is generally based on comparing an approximation of the average product of water (value added per unit of water withdrawn) among industries. It is entirely possible that average products could differ significantly among industries while marginal products might be equal, thus precluding the possibility of income gains from such transfers. Definitive conclusions on the efficiency of such transfers will probably have to await comprehensive research aimed at estimating the average and marginal product functions of water by industry. However, it is generally agreed that agricultural users could not pay the going nonagricultural price of water, suggesting that there is a disparity water productivity at the margin. If that is the case, income could be increased by a different allocation of water resources.

Another conceptual problem arises when estimating actual consumption of water. Unlike many other inputs, the same water used by one producer may be reused by another, so that there can be large differences between withdrawal and consumptive use. Although the measurement problems are particularly severe, it has been estimated that the ratio of consumptive use to fresh water withdrawal is greater for agriculture (0.56) than for either municipal uses (0.22) or self-supplied industrial water (0.03).[4] This makes the agricultural/nonagricultural pricing dichotomy appear even more conducive to inefficiency.

Estimates of actual water consumption would have to include the consumption associated with pollution. With such consumption accounted for, the ratio of consumptive use to withdrawal would probably increase in all three user categories listed above. It is likely that water pollution will be gradually brought under control, resulting in either a decrease in the quantity of water demanded for pollution abatement or an increase in the supply available for other purposes, depending on the viewpoint taken. The reduction in the quantity demanded for waste disposal can be implemented by an increase in the price of water used for waste discharge. This is somewhat indirect, since the price is nominally associated with fines for unlawful discharge of effluent or a tax on discharge. In

[a]The debate among Young and Martin, Campbell, and Kelso concerning the proposed Central Arizona Project to create additional supplies in that area summarizes the significant issues and principles in this allocation and pricing problem.[3]

those places where such pollution is subject to extremely heavy criminal charges, the price of water for this purpose might be considered as infinite.

An idea that has been particularly influential in clouding a meaningful view of water as an economic resource is that there are a set of requirements for water rather than a set of demand functions. Estimates of water supplies necessary for future industrial consumption often are computed as the product of current water withdrawal per unit of output and a projection of output. Implicitly, it is assumed that there will be no substitution of other inputs for water, or vice versa. Such substitution possibilities would imply a range of water requirements for a given output level depending on the price of that input—in other words, it would imply the existence of a demand function. The failure to view water as a conventional resource is at least partially a result of the "water-is-different" syndrome[b] which leads to serious misconceptions about the role to be played by water, how it should be priced, and the way it should be made available for consumption. Many of these problems stem from the fact that water is among the most social of all commodities. Everybody must consume it, and it has customarily been almost a human right to have it available without direct cost. In addition, many uses do not entail consumption and, therefore, externalities are very prevalent, which means that the market may have limited usefulness in producing an optimal allocation.

In summary, while this study is focused on the development implications of water investment, it is important that the characteristics of the resource be understood, especially the nature of demand for water and the pricing system used to allocate it. Capital investments are often called for to alleviate illusory water shortages which might best be overcome by reallocating existing supplies through a more realistic price system. Failure to properly allocate existing water has occurred because of a tradition of viewing water resources in a non-economic and sometimes emotional way. Changing the usual perception of water to one based on economics principles will probably be a prerequisite to approaching efficiency with respect to water resource allocation.

Potential Changes in Water Demand
and Supply

The importance of water investment for future regional economic growth will depend on differential changes in the supply and demand functions for various types of water resources. If changes in technology and consumer

---

[b]Kelso [5] presents a most interesting and enlightening article on this subject. He argues that there exist a number of false images of water, which have had a significant influence on the nature of public policies and institutions, established to guide and control water development and allocation. Thus, it is not surprising that less than optimal use of these resources has resulted.

preferences lead to increases in effective supply and/or decreases in demand, thus reducing or eliminating the scarcity problem (assuming there is one now), it would follow that water investment would probably be a poor tool for stimulating regional growth. Each of the following could have a significant effect on the supply or demand function for water resources, and will be discussed in turn: (1) changes in those technical conditions of production which involve the use of water; (2) changes in waste control and treatment by industry, municipalities, and individuals; (3) changes in consumer income, available leisure time, and preferences; and (4) expanding technology in such fresh water creating activities as desalinization and cloud seeding. Of necessity, the analysis must suggest a set of possibilities, rather than being definitive.

Technical Conditions of Production

It is difficult to estimate true water consumption per unit of output because data indicating industrial withdrawal of water is insufficient to estimate direct consumptive use, and data on water consumption associated with waste disposal (i.e., pollution) is generally unavailable. What evidence there is indicates divergent trends. For example, Bower points out that modernization of steam power plants and increasing complexity of petroleum refineries have resulted in increased use of water per unit of output, while in production of pulp and paper consumptive use per unit has decreased (although gross water applied has increased) and waste loads for that industry have declined.[6] These divergent trends are largely explained by the fact that changes in consumptive use of water per unit of output have been stimulated by factors other than water cost or availability. That is, the objective of minimizing labor or raw materials costs has led to changes in production techniques which require greater or lesser amounts of water, but, as the latter accounts for an insignificant part of total costs, there has been no general pattern of decreased water use. There is a suggestion here that water may not be a very important productive input, and, hence, its development may not stimulate industrial growth.

Water supply and quantities demanded in production are not independent. Changes in supply, if they lead to significant price changes, may cause changes in production techniques that will be water saving or water using, depending on whether price increased or decreased.[c] Alternatively, changes in requirements will have an effect on the quantity available to other uses. Although the available evidence is insufficient to predict the trend in water requirements in production,

---

[c]For most industries, however, large changes in the price of water would probably not lead to material changes in the method of production. What is needed is a set of empirically estimated production and water demand functions for each relevant industry, so that elasticities of demand and substitution could be estimated and used to predict changing factor proportions.

it is clear that changes therein, particularly in agriculture, have important implications for the entire question of water availability. For example, Leven argues that reducing irrigation use of water in California by five percent would more than double the amount of water available to the Los Angeles metropolitan area.[7] Young and Martin make a similar case for reallocation of water in Arizona, where 90 percent of consumption is accounted for by crop irrigation.

> Thus, evidence does not show Arizona's water problem to be a physical shortage of water or a rapidly collapsing agricultural sector due to the groundwater overdraft. Arizona's real problem lies in allocating its available water so as to maintain a high rate of economic growth.[8]

Waste Treatment and Control

Growing public concern over water pollution can be expected to result in more comprehensive legislation at all government levels, greatly restricting the practice of indiscriminate dumping of wastes into waterways. The imposition of fines and/or charges for some forms of waste disposal will result in industries and municipalities increasing the extent of waste treatment, so that what is discharged is more readily decomposed and nonpolluting. In some areas, this is already an accomplished fact,[9] while in others progress is just now beginning. The trend, however, is clear and well-established; pollution from the present kinds and levels of production is going to be diminished.

Such controls not only increase the availability of fresh water, they can also result in the development of water for recreational purposes. Cleaned-up rivers and lakes may allow fishing, boating, swimming, etc., in areas where they were previously unavailable. Benefits accrue to area residents both in the form of the utility derived from consuming these recreational resources and, to the extent tourists are attracted, the income associated with tourist expenditures. The growing awareness of pollution problems and the emphasis on their correction has resulted in many industrial plants spending significantly more for waste treatment than for direct water intake. Bower [10] cites examples of specific case studies of waste disposal costs for a variety of industries, including steel, petroleum refining, and chemical manufacturing.

Income, Leisure, and Consumer Preferences

A trend toward increasing income, population, and leisure time has resulted in greatly increased demand for recreational and tourist services. This is manifest by congestion in the better known state and national parks and in the rapid growth of private recreational and tourist facilities. As a number of recreational activities are water-oriented (e.g., fishing, boating, swimming, etc.), there have been significant increases in the use of many rivers and lakes for these purposes. Generally, water-based recreational activities involve nonconsumptive use of the resource, except for some water pollution problems which are probably minor when compared with those associated with municipal and industrial waste disposal.

Increased recreational use of existing lakes, rivers, streams, etc., should not result in a significant increase in the consumptive use of water, and, indirectly, it may be a factor in developing new supplies.[d] Inclusion of secondary benefits from recreational use in a benefit-cost analysis for a water project might be sufficient to justify its construction, whereas primary and secondary benefits exclusive of those associated with recreation would not be. As discussed earlier, water resources suitable for recreational use could also be an important factor in the development of the region's tourist industry.

Increasing urbanization of the population has implications for water consumption. Higher population densities in the larger cities, implying smaller yards and gardens than in smaller cities and rural areas, should be reflected in lower per capita water consumption. Increased importance of multifamily housing in virtually all areas of the country may tend to reduce per capita consumption. This must be adjusted for the trend toward high-rise buildings surrounded by large open spaces or recreation areas that might be heavy water users, although the per capita use would probably be lower than in the low density suburban or nonurban areas.

Technology in Fresh Water Creation

Future supplies of fresh water may be augmented by such activities as desalinization of sea water and cloud seeding. While there have been important advances in desalinization technology, for most areas water costs associated with desalinization are still too high to offer a real alternative to the more conventional sources.[11] The plants that have been built in the United States (such as those at Roswell, New Mexico; Point Loma, California; and New Orleans) are primarily experimental, although the installations at St. Croix in the Virgin Islands and Guantanamo Bay, Cuba, are fulfilling a real need. As of 1965, total installed capacity of desalting plants was in excess of 300 million gallons per day (GPD) compared to capacity of 80 million GPD ten years earlier.

Recent developments using membrane systems, rather than the more conventional distillation systems, indicate that for large plants (several million

---

[d]If the form of a water resource is changed to facilitate certain recreational activities, such as in spreading the water from a free flowing stream into a large reservoir, losses from evaporation will indeed be significant. Clearly, this evaporation should be viewed as consumption by recreational users.

GPD) the cost of desalting sea water may fall as low as $0.25 per thousand gallons, or roughly $81 per acre-foot. Although far too high for most agricultural uses, this rate could be paid by many industrial and municipal users. These are significant economies of scale present, as plants using the same technology but having a capacity of one million GPD result in costs of approximately $1.00 per thousand gallons or $325 per acre-foot, which is probably not competitive.[12]

Another possible alternative source of water supply is from Antarctic icebergs. More than two-thirds of the earth's fresh water supply lies in these icebergs. Schemes have been suggested that would use atomic powered tugboats to tow trains of icebergs up to 50 miles long to the coast off southern California, where ten foot chunks would be put into an underwater pipe that would carry them to land. The icebergs would be covered by plastic to reduce loss due to melting to roughly 10 percent. Not only would this water be significantly purer than the aqueduct water now being supplied to southern California, but initial estimates place the delivered cost at roughly $25 per acre-foot compared to $65 per acre-foot for aqueduct water.[13]

Although all of these radical departures from traditional water supply activities must still be considered somewhat experimental, their potential impact must be given consideration. Furthermore, it is likely that other technological developments in the future could radically alter both the supply and demand functions for water.

Summary

While increasing population and industrialization may be expected to lead to greater total water withdrawal, there are a number of trends that will influence both the demand and available supply. This discussion has been quite general and would not allow definitive predictions to be made concerning future water usage. The purpose is to emphasize that the impact of water investment on regional economic activity will depend on relative demand and supply, and that both of the latter may change significantly as a result of the trends and developments just described. Rational policies for water investment can only be determined after the effects of the above factors have been analyzed

Notes

1. Harvey S. Perloff and Lowdon Wingo, Jr., "Natural Resource Endowment and Regional Economic Growth," in Proceedings of *Conference on Natural Resources and Economic Growth* (Ann Arbor: University of Michigan, 1960).

2. Charles W. Howe and William K. Easter, *Interbasin Transfers of Water: Economic Issues and Impacts* (Baltimore: The Johns Hopkins Press, 1971) p. 7.
3. See: Robert A. Young and William E. Martin, "The Economics of Arizona's Water Problem," *Arizona Review*, XVI, 15 (March, 1967) 9–18.
   George W. Campbell, "Comments on 'The Economics of Arizona's Water Problem', An Article by Young and Martin," (Mimeo., Department of Agricultural Economics, The University of Arizona, Tucson, Arizona, March 27, 1967).
   Maurice M. Kelso, "An Appraisal of Comments by Dr. George W. Campbell, dated March 27, 1967, on an article by Drs. Young and Martin entitled 'The Economics of Arizona's Water Problem'," (Mimeo., Department of Agricultural Economics, The University of Arizona, Tucson, Arizona, June 21, 1967).
4. See: C. Richard Murray, *Estimated Water Use in the United States, 1965*, Circular 556 (Washington, D.C.: U.S. Geological Survey, 1968).
5. Maurice M. Kelso, "The Water is Different Syndrome or What is Wrong with the Water Industry," (paper presented at the American Water Resource Association Meetings, San Francisco, November, 1967).
6. See: Blair T. Bower, "Industrial Water Utilization: Substitution Possibilities and Regional Water Resources Development," (paper presented at the annual meeting of the Western Section, Regional Science Association, Tempe, Arizona, February 6–8, 1964).
   Blair T. Bower, "The Economics of Industrial Water Utilization," in Allen V. Kneese and Stephen C. Smith, eds., *Water Research* (Baltimore: The Johns Hopkins Press, 1966).
7. Charles L. Leven, "A Framework for the Evaluation of Secondary Impacts of Public Investment," *American Journal of Agricultural Economics*, LII, 5 (December, 1970) 723–729.
8. Young and Martin, "The Economics of Arizona's Water Problem," p. 13.
9. The Willamette River in Oregon is an excellent example. See: Ethel A. Starbird, "A River Restored: Oregon's Willamette," *National Geographic*, CXLI, 6 (June, 1972) 816–835.
10. Bower, "The Economics of Industrial Water Utilization."
11. For a concise summary of desalinization techniques see: J.W. McCutchan and Walter M. Pollit, "Sea Water Conversion: Its Potential and Problems," in Kneese and Smith, eds., *Water Research*, pp. 423–437.
12. See: Aqua-Chem, Inc., *Aqua-Chem MESF Evaporators: A New Desalting Technology For the Water Needs of the '70's* (Waukesha, Wisconsin: Auqa-Chem, 1971).
13. See: "The Iceberg Cometh," *Newsweek*, LXXX, 8 (August 21, 1972) 45–46.

6 Water Resources and Regional Growth

The Importance of Water in Industrial Activities

In this chapter consideration is given to the relative importance of water in the productive process, and the alternative ways that water may enter the production function. An attempt will also be made to identify those industries wherein water might be an important input, in the sense of accounting for a significant part of the total production cost structure. The material presented in this section will provide an essential background for the analysis of specific types of water resource investments in different regional economies.

Water investment might influence industrial activity in one or more ways. Illustrative of these ways are a reduction in production costs associated with lower prices for water intake, reduced charges for waste discharge, and/or reduction in energy costs as a result of low-cost hydroelectric power generation. Depending on the importance of these factors in the production process and the elasticities of the factor demand functions, relative substitution of water for other inputs could result in increased marginal products for other factors including labor and private capital.

By increasing water availability in "water short" areas, the possibility that such shortages are placing a limit on levels of population and economic activity is reduced. It is difficult to estimate the importance of this factor because the measurement of water supply (both quality and quantity) is sometimes nebulous, particularly with regard to ground water, and the existence of many water-saving possibilities in both production and consumption. A simple economic framework for evaluating alternative possibilities is outlined later in this chapter.

Investments that allow relatively low cost shipment of commodities over water increase the range of producer choice with respect to transportation alternatives. If such transport is used, the average per unit transport cost of goods shipped, both into and out of the region, should be at least as low as before the investment. As transportation costs are an important part of the total cost structure for some industries, the development of water transportation could be an important stimulant to attracting new industry, i.e., it can significantly influence the relative input-output access of the region, perhaps more so than the factors discussed above.

Certain large-scale projects may provide recreational facilities and/or other amenities for both residents and tourists. Such investments tend to increase welfare levels of residents by expanding their range of choice in consumption. Such investment may also stimulate incremental tourist activity sufficient to provide the basis for the development of a new or expanded export industry for the region.

This analysis begins by considering the way in which water enters the production function. It will be useful to think of two types of industries, one where water enters directly, and in significant amounts, into the productive process, and the other where water is quite incidental to actual production, (e.g., where it is used primarily for drinking and sanitary purposes).[a] Assume the following production function for a firm:

$$Y = A(t) N^\alpha K_0^{\beta_0} K_1^{\beta_1} \ldots K_p^{\beta_p} \qquad (6\text{-}1)$$

where Y represents output, $A(t)$ is a shift parameter which adjusts the function for technical change (the latter assumed to be a function of time), N represents labor, and K_0 is the private capital stock. $K_1, \ldots, K_p$ are social overhead capital inputs which can be separated into two classes. $K_1, \ldots K_n$ contribute directly to the production process, and $K_{n+1}, \ldots K_p$ contribute only indirectly in the sense that their existence is necessary but changing their quantities will not materially affect output levels (i.e., the values of $\beta_{n+1}, \ldots, \beta_p$ are probably close to zero). α and the β_i are nonnegative parameters.

The production function might be written as

$$Y = [A(t) N^\alpha K_0^{\beta_0} K_1^{\beta_1} \ldots K_p^{\beta_p}] \, \delta \qquad (6\text{-}2)$$

where

$$\delta = \begin{cases} 0 \text{ if } \bar{K} < M \\ 1 \text{ if } \bar{K} \geqslant M \end{cases}$$

$\bar{K}$ is a vector of indirect social capital inputs $(K_{n+1}, \ldots, K_p)$ and $\bar{M}$ is a vector of minimum requirements for production to take place.

---

[a]Tolley [1] identifies five water-oriented manufacturing industries: food and food products, wood and wood products, chemicals, petroleum, and primary metals. In Garrison's study of the Tennessee Valley,[2] analysis at the three digit (SIC) level identified representatives of the lumber and wood products; stone, clay, glass, and concrete products; textiles; paper and allied products; and fabricated metal products industries, in addition to those identified by Tolley, as being water-oriented. In the Garrison study, industries are considered as water-oriented if they rank in the upper quartile of industries ranked by gallons of water withdrawn per dollar added. It is possible that even for these industries, water costs may still be insignificant, as is shown later in the text.

Using Equation (6-1), the profit function for the firm is given by

$$\pi = P \left[A(t) N^{\alpha} K_0^{\beta_0} K_1^{\beta_1} \ldots K_p^{\beta_p} \right] - W N - \sum_{i=1}^{n} r_i K_i - \sum_{i=n+1}^{p} \tilde{r}_i K_i \qquad (6\text{-}3)$$

where P is the output price per unit, W is the wage rate, and the r are the prices of capital. A tilde will be used to denote the price of an indirect social capital input. The well-known first order conditions for a profit maximum require that

$$\partial \pi / \partial N = P \left(\partial Y / \partial N \right) - W = 0$$

$$\partial \pi / \partial K_i = P \left(\partial Y / \partial K_i \right) - r_i = 0, i = 1, \ldots, n \qquad (6\text{-}4)$$

$$\partial \pi / \partial K_i = P(\partial Y / \partial K_i) - \tilde{r}_i = 0, i = n + 1, \ldots, p$$

or that inputs be employed until their marginal value products equal their respective prices.

For industries in the low water intensity class (e.g., trade, transportation, and printing and publishing), it is likely that water accounts for such a small proportion of total costs that the water cost per unit of output is effectively zero. For these industries, there should be no perceptible direct effect on water consumption, output levels, or factor returns associated with water investment that increases available supply and/or lowers per unit water prices. There remains the possibility that those industries will feel indirect effects of water investment to the extent that they are linked with the water-intensive industries that are directly influenced.

Those industries where water is a significant input will be characterized by a production elasticity (β_i) for the water input significantly different from zero. For these industries, a decrease in the price of water should lead to substitution of water for other inputs, at least initially. If K_2 represents water, and if, because of a reduction in its price or an increase in available supply, more water is used, the marginal product of labor,

$$\partial Y / \partial N = \alpha A(t) N^{\alpha-1} K_0^{\beta_0} K_1^{\beta_1} K_2^{\beta_2} \ldots K_p^{\beta_p} \qquad (6\text{-}5)$$

will increase as K_2 increases. Clearly, the marginal products of all other inputs will increase, and, if β_2 is zero or near zero, as in most water-extensive industries, the magnitude of K_2 will be immaterial. But if water accounts for a large share of total costs, and if the firm faces a budget constraint, output can be increased by reduction in the price of water.

Although the foregoing framework is technically correct, it is possible that few if any nonagricultural industries view water costs as significant. If that is the case, the impacts just described are unlikely to occur, except possibly in the agriculture sectors. Consider the following hypothetical example. Assume that all water-oriented industries purchase their entire water requirements from a very modern desalinization plant at $0.25 per thousand gallons (approximately $81 per acre-foot). Clearly, this is a gross overstatement of true water costs to industry. First, about 80 percent of industrial water is self-supplied, and second, that which is purchased generally costs less than the prices assumed above.[b] The purpose here is to show that even under conditions of extremely high water prices, water costs still tend to be insignificant for most industries (excluding agriculture). In Table 6-1, the 25 water-oriented industries, as identified by Garrison,[4] are listed, together with a measure of relative water consumption and water costs as a percentage of value added, under the alternative assumptions that either all water is purchased from a single municipal supplier or that 80 percent of the water withdrawal is self-supplied with the remainder being purchased.

Examination of the data indicates that, even under the high water cost assumption, only twelve industries would have water costs in excess of five percent of value added. It is unlikely that under such conditions production techniques would be changed to sharply reduce water withdrawal. Using the more reasonable conditions of the second assumption, in only one industry does water account for more than five percent of value added.

In another case, Bower [5] estimated total water utilization costs (including waste control expenses) at less than three percent of the cost per kwh of electricity produced in a steam electric plant. Thus, even for these industries that are generally thought of as heavy users of water, the annual increment in labor costs is probably greater than the total amount spent on water.

At this point, a very tentative conclusion that water costs to industry other than agriculture probably are not of primary importance can be made. Clearly, large quantities of water per dollar of output are withdrawn by some industries, but there would appear to be a sufficient number of low-cost water sources (including recycling) to render water a relatively insignificant input. If water cost is not important to most industries, it should not be a significant factor in the industrial location decision. It will, nevertheless, be useful to look more closely at the nature of these decisions, with particular reference given to the role played by water.

The possibility that limited supplies of water or water-based services may

_____

[b]Clarke [3] estimates that water prices to industry range from $7 to $82 per acre-foot for direct water supply, and that recycled water costs industry $3 to $16 per acre-foot. The price assumed above would be at the upper end of the direct water supply price range.

Table 6-1

Water Cost Relative to Value Added, Water-Oriented Manufacturing Industries

Industry	SIC Code	Water Withdrawal per Dollar of Value Added (gallons)	Water Cost as a Percent of Value Added*	
			Assumption 1**	Assumption 2†
Pulp mills	261	1,094	27.0%	5.4%
Paper mills, except building	262	656	16.4	3.3
Basic chemicals	281	583	14.6	2.9
Steel rolling and finishing	331	528	13.2	2.6
Paperboard mills	263	526	13.2	2.6
Agricultural chemicals	287	479	12.0	2.4
Petroleum refining	291	472	11.8	2.4
Sugar	206	461	11.5	2.4
Primary nonferrous metals	333	429	10.7	2.1
Sawmills and planing mills	242	404	10.1	2.0
Gum and wood chemicals	286	338	8.5	1.7
Building paper and board mills	266	244	6.1	1.2
Fibers, plastics, rubbers	282	196	4.9	1.0
Miscellaneous chemical products	289	176	4.4	0.9
Cement hydraulic	324	173	4.3	0.8

*Water from the municipal desalinization plant is assumed to be sold at $0.25 per thousand gallons.

**All water is purchased from a single municipal supplier.

†Eighty percent of water is self-supplied at costs that would usually be less than $0.05 per thousand gallons; 20 percent is purchased at a price somewhat less than the upper limit of $0.25 per thousand gallons used in Assumption 1.

Source: Charles B. Garrison, *Effect of Water Resources on Economic Growth in the Tennessee Valley Region* (Knoxville: University of Tennessee, 1971).

place a ceiling on regional production or population levels was mentioned earlier. Given existing production techniques, water consumption habits of individuals, and demand for regional output, it is conceivable that the water supply in a given region may not be sufficient. Shortages are likely to be seasonal in nature, occurring primarily during the summer months when rainfall is minimal, losses due to evaporation are high, and consumption is increased due to field crop, lawn, and garden irrigation. These shortages are likely to result in seasonal changes in consumption, particularly in nonindustrial uses. Production processes involving water consumption probably cannot be altered as easily as human consumption habits, particularly those associated with nonper-

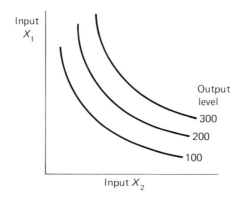

Figure 6-1. Hypothetical Input-Input Relationships.

sonal uses. Recurring shortages will tend to lead to restrictions on the use of
water for certain purposes: water-saving changes in productive processes and
individual consumption habits; investment to create new supplies; firms and
individuals moving to other regions to escape the problem; establishment
of a different pricing schedule to better allocate existing supplies, and/or
modification of institutions, both formal and informal, which hold water in low
value uses.[c] Of these, the investment alternative often is the one suggested by
local interests; the last two alternatives might be optimal in many cases. It is
unlikely that either firms or individuals will adopt water-saving methods unless
there is economic pressure to do so, which might take the form of higher
prices for water during periods of shortage.

Let us consider the water shortage problem in an economic framework
which may be useful in estimating the value of water in alternative uses and in
evaluating the possibility of substituting other inputs for water. Assume, for
simplicity, that there are two inputs, X_1 (water) and X_2 (other resources).
A given level of output can be produced with various combinations of X_1 and
X_2, as shown in Figure 6-1. The shape of the isoquants of production may
vary in different situations. One extreme would be a straight line connecting the
two axes, which would indicate complete substitutability between the inputs.
The opposite extreme would be a point representing each quantity of production. This alternative is equivalent to the concept of a water requirement, i.e.,
that there is only one way to produce.

Isoquants of the type shown in Figure 6-1 have the expected shape, which
indicates diminishing marginal productivity for both resources as applications
are increased. However, in many situations the mix of inputs is not varied
in extremely small increments (for reasons such as the fact that a whole water
project must be developed, or none at all). Thus, smooth curves for isoquants are

---

[c]Empirical evidence of increased water resource values which can result from institutional change is presented by Gardner and Fullerton.[6]

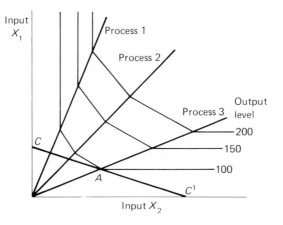

Figure 6-2. Hypothetical Input-Input Relationships with Three Discrete Processes.

sometimes expected, but in other cases the isoquants have discrete linear segments dictated by the finite number of fixed processes available. The isoquants are then as shown in Figure 6-2 in which three processes are available for producing any of the three output levels. Process 1 uses a maximum amount of the water resource. Process 3 uses a maximum of the other resource. By adding isocost lines (or budget lines) the criterion for selection of the best process is available. Let CC' in Figure 6-2 represent a fixed amount of expenditure that can be divided in any way so as to be consistent with the prices of X_1 and X_2. If water (X_1) were to become cheaper relative to the other input, the slope of CC' would become steeper, so that a method of production other than Process 3 at Point A may become best. Furthermore, since one of the resources is cheaper, the limited budget can now buy more resources (assuming a fixed budget). Thus, a higher output level can be expected.

Certain portions of the isoquant field may be unfeasible. That is, if there are limits on availability of one of the resources, any process which exceeds such a limit is not a valid option. It should be recognized that this type of analysis would lead to values being attached to some resources as they might replace others and as they relieve the binding constraints on production. These concepts are usually applied empirically by using the linear programming technique and associated concepts as discussed in Chapter 10.

The Location Decision: Industrial
and Individual

Both the shift-share technique for identifying sources of employment change and the export base growth theory place emphasis on the ability of a region to compete for an increasing share of national industrial growth, particularly in those sectors where output will be exported from the region. Many state and local industrial-economic development agencies also view attracting new industry as the primary source of growth, and some devote a large share of their resources to promotional rather than investment-type activities. In Chapter 2 it was argued that this is a rather narrow view of the regional growth process, as it fails to identify the more fundamental sources of growth, such as increases in the supply and quality of productive factors, especially labor. However, it cannot be denied that decisions made in the private sector by firms seeking new plant locations play a role in regional growth, and, therefore, an analysis of that decision process, with particular emphasis on the role played by water resources, is important.

However, the importance of human location decisions cannot be neglected. Borts and Stein [7] argue, in direct opposition to the export-base theory, that shifts in labor supply schedules are more a determinant of shifts in the location of manufacturing activity than the latter are a determinant of the former. They claim that the tendency for jobs to go where there are potential employees is greater than for people to go where employment opportunities exist. This conclusion is supported by most studies of the industrial location decision, which indicate that availability of labor is almost invariably one of the most important factors in that decision. Muth [8] brings the debate to its logical conclusion by arguing, with supporting empirical evidence, that employment and migration are simultaneously determined; an increase in one will lead to multiple increases in both. In view of this, the location decision of both the individual and the firm and the impact of water resource development thereon must be considered.

Although nonpecuniary factors sometimes are important, a firm typically seeks that location that will result in maximum profit.[9] Given a set of location specific revenues (R) and costs (C) and m location alternatives, the one which maximizes the profit (π) function,

$$\pi_i = R_i - C_i, i = 1, \ldots, m \tag{6-6}$$

is selected. If revenue is invariant with respect to location (i.e., $R_i = \bar{R}$ for all i), then the problem is one of selecting that location that minimizes costs.

It is appropriate to separate the problem into a macrolocation decision, the selection of a rather large region such as the Pacific coast, and a micro-decision, the selection of the specific site within that region. The macrodecision is usually based on revenue considerations, i.e., the desire to better serve and thereby capture a larger share of a regional market, although examples of interregional movement of firms to take advantage of low costs are not unknown. The movement of textile producers from New England to the south is a case in point. It is claimed that the microdecision tends to be dominated by cost factors, particularly those associated with labor and transportation, although empirical support for this assertion is sketchy. It is likely that water cost and availability would enter only the latter decision, if at all. Based on earlier analysis, it appears that, for most industries, water as a direct production input may not be an important factor in the location of industry at either the macro- or microlevel.

Examination of industrial location studies does not indicate water or water-related services to be a primary locational factor. Many of these studies do not even mention water as a factor. Either it was not sufficiently important to the researcher, given the purposes of that study, to be included, or it was not indicated as being significant by those industrialists surveyed. In general, the existence of certain types of water resources in a region is a consideration to some industries, but in very few cases is it a critical or even primary factor.

Greenhut and Colbert,[10] in a survey of 1,294 new plants and expansions in Florida, inquired into the importance of three water-related factors: electric power costs,[d] adequate supply and quality of water, and adequate waste disposal facilities. In selecting the state (the macrolocation decision), power cost was an important factor to 15 firms, water supply was important to only 1 firm, and 17 companies mentioned waste disposal facilities as being important. In selecting the community (the microdecision), water-related factors were important to only 11 of the 1,294 firms. Unless these resources are available throughout Florida in adequate quantities and qualities at similar prices, which is not likely, we must conclude they were unimportant in the decision as to whether to locate in that state, and, if so, where in the state.

Mueller, Wilken, and Wood [11], in a study of the industrial location decision in Michigan, reported that firms accounting for 41 percent of total employment covered by the survey mentioned water as an important locational factor. In the primary metals, rubber, plastics, petroleum, and chemical products sectors, more than 50 percent of the respondents included water as being important. However, in all sectors, the number of firms indicating labor costs, labor availability, and proximity to markets as important was significantly higher than the number who mentioned water.

There are two other studies that should be given brief mention. Boblett,[12] in a survey of industrial realtors, estimated that the adequacy of water, sewers, utilities, gas, electric power, etc., ranked seventh in importance as a locational factor, and was considered of secondary importance. In the *Fortune* magazine survey [13] of industrial location practices of one thousand of the country's largest companies, it was found that water supply, cost of power and utilities, and transportation by water ranked seventh, eighth, and ninth respectively. Each of these was mentioned by about 30 percent of those firms responding.

The relative unimportance of water in the industrial location decision,

---

[d]Clearly, electric power need not be water related. In Florida hydroelectric power generation would probably be quite rare.

as indicated by its omission from consideration in many analyses and its
secondary rank in others, is concisely explained by Bower: [14]

> That water is a relatively unimportant factor in location decisions
> appears to stem primarily from the flexibility inherent in industrial
> water utilization systems, and in the fact that water utilization costs are
> a relatively small proportion of both total plant investment costs and
> total production costs, particularly for the heavy water-using/polluting
> industries.

The individual is a utility maximizer, and will select that location which
maximizes his utility function. However, everyone is initially located somewhere,
say Point A, and a move to any other location involves costs and the disutility
associated with moving. Therefore, a move from A to any alternative location,
say B, will occur only if

$$U_B > U_A + DU_{AB} \tag{6-7}$$

That is, the move will take place only if the level of utility at B (U_B) is greater
than the sum of utility at $A(U_A)$ and the disutility of moving (DU_{AB}), the
latter defined to include money costs. Of m possible locations, the potential
migrant will select the one which maximizes the measure of net utility (Z)
as given by the function

$$Z = U_j - U_A - DU_{Aj}, j = 1, \ldots, m \tag{6-8}$$

It is likely, of course, that a maximum will occur at A, in which case there is no
move.

The utility function will depend on a number of variables, including
employment opportunities; climate; living costs; housing availability and quality;
public service quality, particularly in education; and cultural opportunities.
For a subset of the potential migrants, water resources, particularly those for
recreation, might be significant, but for the vast majority of people it is doubtful
that water is an important consideration. Household consumption of water
would rarely account for more than two or three percent of the family budget,
and, therefore, differential prices for water among cities or regions would be
unimportant. In the limiting case where water quality is very poor, water might
play a more important role.

If the location of people induced industrial location, and if water resources
attracted people to an area, then an indirect link could be established between
water resource development and the location of industry. Although there is
evidence in support of the first premise, there is little empirical basis for the
second. Therefore, if water does attract industry it must do it more directly,

through entry into the production function, and, as suggested above, there are few industries where water is an important factor of production.

The Sequence of Developmental Impacts

If water resource development is effective in inducing economic development, there must be a process that occurs between the time the project is begun and the time the developmental impacts take effect. The identification of the sequence of microchanges in the regional economy is essential to an understanding of the way investment by the public sector might influence economic development.

The process of economic growth in a region following a water resource development is seen as a sequence of six phases:

1. Resource development (i.e., the creation of regional activity potential)
2. Changes in relative factor productivities in both the project region and other affected areas
3. A broadening of the range of producer and consumer choice
4. Intra- and interregional movement of capital and labor
5. Direct and indirect forward and backward linkage effects
6. Second order impacts associated with agglomeration and scale economies and the attainment of minimum threshold levels for development of certain specialized activities

These phases are not necessarily independent; they tend to reinforce as well as to occur serially. The failure of one phase to occur may reduce or eliminate the possibility of another occurring. Furthermore, the phases are not discrete in time—effects associated with phase one may still be taking place when phase five or six is beginning. There is, however, a rough temporal ordering of the sequence.

For a region to experience complete development potential (i.e., to experience all six phases), the economic size of the project would probably have to be large relative to the size of the regional economy. Also, the project may have to provide a range of water-oriented services rather than being a single-purpose project if maximum development is induced. For purposes of the following discussion, it is assumed that the project is a major one producing services in each of the following areas: hydroelectric power; flood control; increased supply of water for agriculture, industry, and households; transportation; and recreation. This list is essentially an enumeration of the types of resource development that constitute the first phase of the development sequence.

Flood control will increase the supply of occupiable or productive land for a variety of uses. In most cases, eliminating or reducing the threat of flood should reduce the variance and increase the expected value of the income stream accruing to area inhabitants, in addition to reducing the psychic disutility associated with flooding or the mere threat of floods. These changes should make the area a more suitable place for area residents and more attractive to potential in-migrants and new industry. Increased water supply, possibly combined with an increase in quality, represents another developed resource. In cases where water is a direct input, such as in irrigated agriculture, this will affect the region's production function directly. In other cases, such as most municipal and nonindustrial uses, where water is used only indirectly, the increased supplies would not have a significant effect on production. In areas suffering from severe water shortages, increased supplies may raise the ceiling or constraint on production and population associated with this limited resource. Other major resources developed include the availability of hydroelectric power, possibly at reduced cost, and a new transportation alternative in the form of a navigable river. As discussed below, the latter may have rather significant impacts on factor productivity, and, therefore, on production costs as well as on distribution costs. Finally, the reservoirs, rivers, and/or streams created or controlled as a result of the project may provide an important set of recreational resources. This development will not only provide utility to area residents, but also to nonresidents, thus setting the stage for the development or expansion of the region's tourist industry.

Phase two, changes in relative factor productivities, is perhaps the most fundamental, as it will lead to those changes in factor returns and industrial cost structure that are associated with both the interregional movement of people and productive capacity, and increases in the productive capability of existing labor and capital. Given the large-scale project assumed herein, it is likely that costs of power and water will be reduced, at least initially. Furthermore, as certain exports and imports (as well as some intraregional commodity flows) can be shipped via water at low cost, average per unit transport cost for commodities shipped into and out of the region should also be reduced as a result of the availability of water transport. Assuming that regional producers are profit maximizers, the change in relative costs will cause a relative substitution of those inputs whose cost has been reduced for labor and other unaffected inputs. This does not mean that less labor will be hired, only that the ratio of, say, hydropower or water input to labor will be higher. This assumes, of course, that there is some degree of substitution among these factors. Factor returns will influence and be influenced by changes in supplies, and these must be considered in a complete model.

The impact of lower transport costs and relative increases in some non-human inputs can be analyzed in the following model. Assume the region produces only one output (Y) under a Cobb-Douglas production function,[e]

$$Y = A(t) K^{\alpha} N^{1-\alpha}, 0 \leqslant \alpha \leqslant 1 \qquad (6\text{-}9)$$

where $A(t)$ is a shift parameter reflecting neutral (between the inputs) technological progress over time and K and N represent capital and labor respectively.
The marginal products of capital and labor are given by

$$\partial Y/\partial K = \alpha [A(t) (N/K)^{1-\alpha}] \qquad (6\text{-}10)$$

and

$$\partial Y/\partial N = (1-\alpha) [A(t) (K/N)^{\alpha}] \qquad (6\text{-}11)$$

The price received per unit of output by the regional producer (P^R) is equal to the price at the market (P^M) minus the cost of transporting the product from the project area (call it region R) to the market (T^{RM}):

$$P^R = P^M - T^{RM} \qquad (6\text{-}12)$$

Assuming a perfectly competitive market structure, the demand for labor (N_D) is given by the value of the marginal product function,

$$N_D = P^R \cdot MP_N \qquad (6\text{-}13)$$

and making appropriate substitutions,

$$N_D = (P^M - T^{RM}) (1-\alpha) A(t) (K/N)^{\alpha} \qquad (6\text{-}14)$$

Consider a linear labor supply (N_s) function which is dependent on the money wage (W):

$$N_s = a + b\, W, \text{ where } a, b > 0 \qquad (6\text{-}15)$$

While it is clear that significant interregional shifts of labor will affect both the level and slope of the function, assume that both a and b are constant. Now, equating the supply and demand functions,

---

[e]The use of a Cobb-Douglas production function is only for the sake of clarity and ease of exposition. The analysis to follow holds for all functions which are linear and homogeneous, and perhaps for other situations.

$$a + b\,W = (P^M - T^{RM})\,(1 - \alpha)\,A(t)\,(K/N)^{\alpha} \qquad\qquad (6\text{-}16)$$

and solving for W yields a function for the wage rate in the project area:

$$W = \frac{1}{b}\,[(P^M - T^{RM})\,(1 - \alpha)\,A(t)\,(K/N)^{\alpha} - a] \qquad\qquad (6\text{-}17)$$

For the wage rate to be positive it must be

$$(P^M - T^{RM})\,(1 - \alpha)\,A(t)\,(K/N)^{\alpha} > a \qquad\qquad (6\text{-}18)$$

which will be assumed.

It will be useful to consider all relevant partial derivatives of (6-17) and the relationship of water investment thereto:

$$\partial W/\partial P^M = \frac{(1 - \alpha)\,A(t)\,(K/N)^{\alpha}}{b} > 0 \qquad\qquad (6\text{-}19)$$

$$\partial W/\partial (T^{RM}) = \frac{-\,(1 - \alpha)\,A(t)\,(K/N)^{\alpha}}{b} < 0 \qquad\qquad (6\text{-}20)$$

$$\partial W/\partial [A(t)] = \frac{(P^M - T^{RM})\,(1 - \alpha)\,(K/N)^{\alpha}}{b} > 0 \qquad\qquad (6\text{-}21)$$

$$\partial W/\partial (K/N) = \frac{\alpha\,(P^M - T^{RM})\,(1 - \alpha)\,(K/N)^{\alpha-1}}{b} > 0 \qquad\qquad (6\text{-}22)$$

The direct impact of some water resource investments would be on transport costs and the capital-labor ratio (defined broadly to include all nonlabor inputs, including hydropower and water, as capital). The parameters of the labor supply schedule might be influenced if people are attracted to an area because of developed water resources. It is also conceivable that if the investment led to significant urbanization, the rate of technological progress might increase. There is some rather tenuous evidence indicating that technical advancements are assimilated and adopted more rapidly in the urban-industrial complexes. In any event, the postulated signs of the relevant partial derivatives associated with water investment in the region (I^R) are:

$$\frac{\partial\,(T^{RM})}{\partial\,I^R} < 0 \qquad\qquad (6\text{-}23)$$

$$\frac{\partial \, [A(t)]}{\partial \, I^R} > 0 \tag{6-24}$$

$$\frac{\partial \, (K/N)}{\partial \, I^R} > 0 \tag{6-25}$$

Now, using the chain rule for derivation, the signs of the partial impacts of water investment on the return to labor can be determined in the following way:

1. Transport cost

$$(\partial W/\partial I)_{T^{RM}} = \partial W/\partial (T^{RM}) \cdot \partial (T^{RM})/\partial I > 0 \tag{6-26}$$

2. Technical progress

$$(\partial W/\partial I)_{A(t)} = \partial W/\partial \, [A(t)] \cdot \partial \, [A(t)] \, /\partial I > 0 \tag{6-27}$$

3. Capital-labor ratio

$$(\partial W/\partial I)_{K/N} = \frac{\partial W}{\partial A(t)} \cdot \frac{\partial (K/N)}{\partial I} > 0 \tag{6-28}$$

All the water investment impacts work toward increasing the wage rate in the project area. The higher wage rate and probability of increased employment in the region will result in a significant increase in total wage income.

Higher incomes generally imply an increase in the effective range of choice for area residents, which leads directly into the third development phase; but first the possible impact on the agricultural sector must be considered. Increased irrigation water supply at lower cost per unit, flood control, and perhaps some benefits from the new transport will have significant effects on the agricultural sector. Average farm productivity and income should rise, assuming increased output in the project area does not influence commodity prices. The range of choice of crop production should be increased, allowing the farmer greater flexibility in adjusting to changes in market conditions. There should also be a change in the rate of movement of farm owners and workers from agriculture to other sectors, particularly manufacturing. The speed at which resource misallocation is corrected, in the sense of moving from low to higher marginal productivity occupations and/or industries, will be an increasing function of the differential in intersectoral and interoccupational factor returns. In this model, the marginal product of labor will have increased in both agriculture and manufacturing; the question is, where has the greatest relative increase been? The rate of intersectoral factor movement may decrease (increase) if relative returns in agriculture (manufacturing) have increased.[f]

Phase 3, the expansion of range of effective choice for both producers and consumers, follows directly from the previous phase. As shown above, increased marginal productivity of labor should result in generally higher incomes, depending in part on changes in the labor supply function. This will increase the size of the consumer choice space. Furthermore, increased production activity, particularly in the tourist and other water-oriented industries, expands the range of employment alternatives in much the same way that new recreational resources provide a consumer "good" that may have been unavailable previously. Producer choice is widened due to increased supplies and lower costs of certain productive inputs, an additional transportation mode for both raw materials and final output, and additional land as potential industrial sites.

Phase 4 concerns the reaction of labor and capital to this expanded range of choice in the project area, with particular reference to both inter- and intraregional factor movement. In-migrants should be attracted by the higher wage rate and possibly by expanded recreational activities. Producers may be attracted by the low cost power, ample water supplies, and range of transportation alternatives, although the examination of the industrial location decision indicated that no definitive conclusions could be made about this possibility.

Industrial expansion and labor supply increases may be simultaneously determined, implying that a change in either variable will lead to multiple increases in both. For example, changes in either migration or productive capacity may reinforce and lead to changes in the other. Migrants will come to the project area from other regions if the present value of their stream of utility within the project area exceeds the sum of that enjoyed at their first location and the disutility associated with relocation. Further, if it can be assumed that the cost of movement is invariant with respect to the age of the migrant, and that the present value of the stream of utility is a decreasing function of age, then most migrants should tend to be relatively young. If this is the case, the proportion of population in peak earning groups found within the project area will increase relative to other regions.

The altering of relative factor productivities (Phase 2) and the intersectoral and interregional factor movements (Phase 4) will cause significant changes in both the input-output relationships among industries and the level and composition of final sales. Phase 6, which is characterized by agglomeration

---

[f]Again, research has shown that the most rapid decline in agricultural employment occurs in areas characterized by high nonagricultural wage levels and low agricultural productivity. Complementing this finding is the fact that the most rapid increases in nonurban manufacturing employment have been in the low productivity agricultural areas.[15]

and scale economies and the attainment of threshold levels for certain activities, will cause even further change in the regional economic structure.

The increase in population and basic economic activity will generate multiple income effects on the retail, wholesale, and service sectors of both the project area and neighboring regions (Phase 5). These indirect impacts will influence sectors such as raw materials production for regional industries, transport services, specialized business services (legal, financial, data processing, etc.), and government.[g] The extent to which the multiple increases in income will accrue to the project area will depend heavily on the extent to which these tertiary activities are developed in the area, and how much development will occur following project completion.

In a region which had been predominantly nonurban and nonindustrial, there will be substantial leakages to neighboring regions, at least in the early stages of the development impact period. This is particularly true in the case of wholesaling and business services (vis-à-vis retail activity) which are usually found only in at least modest sized urban-industrial settings. On the other hand, if the project area is of the urban-industrial sort, leakages will be minimized, and the full multiplier effect of both the investment itself and the following developmental impacts will accrue to the region.

These leakages will change as the result of scale and agglomeration economies and the achievement of threshold levels, all of which are associated with an expanding scale of population and economic activity (Phase 6). In the nonurban regions many activities (e.g., business services) do not exist because the market is of insufficient size. As the project area grows in economic size, some of these activities become feasible and begin to appear; this changes the interregional linkage between, say, the developing business service and regional industry, and also generates a new set of forward and backward linkages in its own right. An expanded scale of operation in other activities (the substitution of a modern supermarket for the general store, for example) leads to economies which are reflected in lower prices, higher quality, and higher wages in that activity. Such scale economies could probably be captured in such diverse operations as department stores, hotels and motels, transportation, employment services, schools, etc. Finally, the industrial development directly associated with the water investment will attract other, nonwater-oriented industry, which will capture economies by being located in close proximity to other industry. Such agglomeration economies are not restricted to industry, as people tend to locate in heavy concentrations for much the same reason. These agglomeration effects take the form of transfer economies (minimizing the cost of moving goods, people, and communications) and external economies, such as large, flexible labor markets and commercial, financial, and public

---

[g]Input-output techniques are very useful in estimating the direct and indirect effects on each industry. These tools and examples of their application will be outlined in Chapters 9 and 10.

services, which will develop to serve large industrial complexes. All of these should work toward increasing the level of welfare of area residents.

The Interdependence of Construction and Development Impacts [16]

In this section, an effort is made to explore in detail the effects of scale and agglomeration economies within the context of an industrial location model of economic growth. A variant of the industrial location model of urban-regional growth [17] is developed, and used to demonstrate the possibility that because of external economies associated with the development of private activities in a region, and the existence of minimum size thresholds for the appearance of other activities, there are interdependencies among seemingly independent investment impacts. The analysis has implications for appropriate spatial distribution of public investment to promote regional development.

In the introduction to this part of the book, three types of economic impacts associated with water investment were defined. They are the construction impact, the service impact, and the development impact. Leven discounts the importance of the construction impact in the establishment of a national water policy.[18]

> For one thing, methodologically it is simply one part of the general problem of the impact of federal spending on economic stabilization, i.e., its impact on current inflationary or deflationary trends. Moreover, it is much more relevant to the specific timing of water resource development than it is to either the quantitative or geographical dimensions of what ought to be done. In short, while construction impact considerations might and should bear importantly on the question of whether a project should be started "this year" or "delayed for a year or two" in light of the economic situation, they should be important strategic elements in discrete project decision-making. It is not clear that they would or should have any major role in setting forth the dimensions of a national water policy over several decades.

Although Leven's classification of investment impacts is both accurate and useful, his discounting of the role of construction impacts in a national water policy, while including developmental impacts, may not be justifiable. It is entirely possible that construction and developmental impacts are interdependent, at least for some types of investment projects. For example, in some situations certain activities, developmental in character, would not be forthcoming in the absence of significant construction impacts. Essentially, the argument to follow is based on the premise that certain activities will be started in the project area, because the sum of profits expected during both the construction and development period, is above the minimum necessary to induce location in the region, but the profit expected during either but not both of those two periods may be insufficient to attract that activity.

The interdependence between construction and development impacts may be limited to those areas where the investment project is large relative to the economic size of the geographic area that will be affected. In a large, well-developed region (i.e., one characterized by significant urbanization and industrialization) increased activity may largely accrue to labor and business already in the area. In the less well-developed economies, significant increases in new business and population could be expected as a result of the project. The analysis developed here will be more applicable to the latter type of economy.

The industrial location model used here divides economic activity in the project area into four sectors. The importance of each sector will be measured by the level of employment $(N_1, \ldots, N_4)$. It will be useful to consider the characteristics of each with regard to three factors: output orientation (consumer or producer goods); the necessary population threshold for the activity to develop locally, which will serve as an approximation of the degree to which economies of scale are present; and the extent to which the industry can capture economies by being located in close proximity to certain other industries (i.e., the presence of agglomeration economies). The operational characteristics of the hypothetical industry set are outlined below:

Industry	Output Orientation	Population Threshold Level	Agglomeration Economies
1	Consumer	Low	No
2	Consumer	High	No
3	Producer	Low	Yes
4	Producer	High	Yes

Industry 1 would include the lower order retail and service activities such as drug and grocery stores, barber shops, service stations, etc. These activities are typically found in the smallest cities, as the economies of their operations dictate that consumption usually takes place in close proximity to the source of production. The second industry also produces goods and services primarily for consumers, but the products are more specialized and require a larger market for efficient operation. Examples might include newspapers, furniture stores, automobile dealers, etc. The large-scale, multiple-purpose project, for which construction time may be four, five, or more years, probably is a prerequisite for significant increases in the number of and employment in firms in the second industry. It is assumed that neither industry enjoys more than insignificant production economies from being spatially close to other industry.

Industries 3 and 4 produce output primarily, although not exclusively, for other industry. Both are characterized by the ability to lower production costs by locating in the same area with other industry. Industry 3 achieves maximum efficiency at relatively low levels of output, and can operate profitably in a relatively small market. Conversely, the last industry can attain maximum efficiency only from large-scale plants, and, therefore, must locate in rather large, primarily urban labor markets. Most of the output from this industry will be exported from the region, and thus, this sector will be one source for transmitting change in the national economy to the region. Industry 4 will probably be composed primarily of manufacturing firms, where the trade-off between production economies and transportation costs dictates that plants be of relatively large size, and serve an area consisting of at least several labor markets or functional economic areas.

The profit maximizing entrepreneur will locate a store or plant in the project area if the expected profit at that location is greater than at all alternative sites, or at least as great as some minimal level set administratively. For many representatives of Industry 1 and perhaps a few from Industry 2, the expected profit from the construction period alone (assuming a zero profit in the development period) will be sufficient to cause them to locate in the project area. The same is probably true for some industries in the third class, particularly those that will be supplying materials for the project itself. Examples might include cement plants, gravel pits, and certain types of transport services. It is clear that many other activities, largely but not exclusively from Industries 3 and 4, will not be able to earn the required profit during the construction phase, and thus will not locate in the project area unless significant profits can be expected as a result of general development following project completion.

The key point is that for many firms, plant or store location cannot be justified on the basis of the profit expected during either the construction or development phase, but the sum of profits expected from both phases will be sufficient to induce location. These locational decisions result in increased flows of labor and capital to the region, setting off a new round of development. This is the basic reason for arguing that construction and development impacts, at least for large-scale projects, cannot be viewed as being independent.

These concepts can be formalized in the following way. Assume that employment in Industry 1 (N_1) is an increasing function of population (P):

$$N_1 = f_1 (P) \tag{6-29}$$

and that Industry 2 employment is also a function of population, but is subject to a minimum threshold level (P_0):

$$N_2 = \delta f_2 (P), \text{ where } \begin{cases} \delta = 1 \text{ if } P \geqslant P_0 \\ \\ \delta = 0 \text{ if } P < P_0 \end{cases} \tag{6-30}$$

Employment in the producer-oriented industries (3 and 4) will depend on employment levels in all industries, and, in the case of Industry 4, a threshold employment level (N_0):

$$N_3 = f_3 (N_1, \ldots, N_4)$$ (6-31)

$$N_4 = \alpha[f_4 (N_1, \ldots, N_4)], \text{ where } \begin{cases} \alpha = 1 \text{ if } \Sigma N_i \geqslant N_0 \\ \\ \alpha = 0 \text{ if } \Sigma N_i < N_0 \end{cases}$$ (6-32)

For any firm, the expected value of profits associated with locating in the project area is the sum of profits earned during the construction period (π^c — assumed to be known with certainty) and those expected during the development period $\epsilon (\pi^D)$

$$\epsilon (\pi) = \pi^c + \epsilon (\pi^D)$$ (6-33)

All future profits are, of course, discounted appropriately. As suggested above, for some activities, π^c will be sufficient to establish a store or plant in the region. Assume there is a spectrum of development (D), where D varies from 0 to 1. The development spectrum ranges from a complete absence of development ($D = 0$) to "complete" development (perhaps this would be the development of a SMSA-size urban industrial complex) where $D = 1$. There is also a probability density function associated with D that indicates the probability that any particular range of development will occur, $f(D)$, and also a function that associates the profit level in an industry with any development level [$g_i (D)$, $i = 1, \ldots, 4$].

Expected profit in the development stage for Industry i is given by

$$\epsilon (\pi_i^D) = \int_0^1 [f (D) \cdot g_i (D)] \, dD, i = 1, \ldots, 4$$ (6-34)

and profit from both stages by

$$\epsilon (\pi_i) = \pi_i^c + \int_0^1 [f (D) \cdot g_i (D)] \, dD, i = 1, \ldots, 4$$ (6-35)

The most interesting group of firms is that for which

$$\pi^c < M \text{ and } \pi^D < M$$ (6-36)

(where M is the minimum profit required), but where

$$\pi^c + \pi^D \geqslant M$$ (6-37)

It is the existence of these firms and their relationship to the location of other firms that suggests the possibility of the nonindependence of the construction and developmental impacts of public investment projects.

There are, of course, indirect effects associated with the locational decisions. Employment in Industries 3 and 4 depends on employment levels in all industries (i.e., there is simultaneity in these functions), implying that increased employment in either of these industries will lead to multiple increases in both. Furthermore, a more complete specification of the equations in our model might include population as an argument in all employment equations and an equation with population as a function of all classes of employment. Thus, an initial change in either population or employment in any industry would lead to multiple increases in population and employment in all industries.

The theory just outlined has implications for the spatial distribution of water and other public investments designed to accelerate regional economic growth. The growth center strategy for regional development has attracted wide interest among economists.[19] Its proponents view the focusing of public investment programs, in or near those regional centers that offer a viable migration alternative to the large metropolitan cities, and which exhibit sufficient regional dominance, to contribute spread effects to the rural areas and smaller cities in the hinterland. They submit that this plan would be effective in the achievement of a more optimal distribution of the nation's population (i.e., less concentration of the population in the larger cities) and would be a lower-cost alternative to the development of new towns.

In articulating the growth center concept, Hansen has recognized the possibility of interdependencies among public investment projects:[20]

> The balanced growth argument for developing lagging regional economies involves initiating a large number of interdependent projects simultaneously. The principle justification for such action is based on the phenomenon of external economies. It is argued that reluctance by individuals to undertake projects in underdeveloped areas is largely a consequence of the high degree of uncertainty as to whether or not relevant products will find a market. This disincentive would be overcome if numerous projects were undertaken simultaneously; investments which would not be profitable in isolation would become so for the ensemble as a result of mutually-favorable external economies.

The possibility that such interdependencies exist, both within and possibly between the sites of public investments, strengthens the position that efforts to develop regional economies would be well advised to concentrate investments and other development programs in one part of the region, probably the nearest growth center, rather than diffusing such efforts throughout the region, a situation where the possibility of capturing external economies is very slight.

Notes

1. George S. Tolley, ed., *Estimation of First Round and Selected Subsequent Income Effects of Water Resource Investment*, a report submitted to the U.S. Army Corps of Engineers Institute for Water Resources (Springfield, Virginia: Clearinghouse for Federal Scientific and Technical Information, February, 1970).

2. Charles B. Garrison, *Effect of Water Resources on Economic Growth In the Tennessee Valley Region* (Knoxville: University of Tennessee, Department of Economics, January, 1971).

3. F.E. Clarke, "Industrial Re-Use of Water," *Industrial and Engineering Chemistry*, LIV, 2 (February, 1962) 18–27.

4. Garrison, *Effect of Water Resources.*

5. Blair T. Bower, "The Economics of Industrial Water Utilization," in Allen V. Kneese and Stephen C. Smith, eds., *Water Research* (Baltimore: The Johns Hopkins Press, 1966) p. 150.

6. B. Delworth Gardner and Herbert H. Fullerton, "Transfer Restrictions and Misallocation of Irrigation Water," *American Journal of Agricultural Economics*, L, 3 (August, 1968) 556–571.

7. George H. Borts and Jerome L. Stein, *Economic Growth in a Free Market* (New York: Columbia University Press, 1964).

8. Richard F. Muth, "Differential Growth Among Large U.S. Cities," (working paper CWR15, Institute for Urban and Regional Studies, Washington University, St. Louis, Missouri, 1968).

9. Voluminous research has been done in the industrial location field. For examples see: Melvin L. Greenhut, *Microeconomics and the Space Economy* (Chicago: Scott Foresman, 1963).
   Edgar M. Hoover, *The Location of Economic Activity* (New York: McGraw-Hill, 1948).
   Eva Mueller and James Morgan, "Location Decisions of Manufacturers," *American Economic Review*, LII, 2 (May, 1962) 204–217.
   John F. Due, "Studies of the State-Local Tax Influence on Location of Industry," *National Tax Journal*, XIV, 2 (June, 1961) 165–183.
   William C. Lewis, "Tax Incentives and Industrial Location," *Reviews in Urban Economics*, I, 2 (Fall, 1968) 29–51.
   A comprehensive bibliography on this subject has been compiled by the United Nations. See: United Nations Industrial Development Organization, *Industrial Location and Regional Development: An Annotated Bibliography* (New York: United Nations, 1970).

10. Melvin L. Greenhut and Marshall R. Colberg, *Factors in the Location of Florida Industry* (Tallahassee: The University of Florida Press, 1962).

11. Eva Mueller, Arnold Wilkin, and Margaret Wood, *Location Decisions and Industrial Mobility in Michigan* (Ann Arbor: The University of Michigan Press, 1961).

12. Robert P. Boblett, "Factors in Industrial Location," *The Appraisal Journal*, XXXV, 4 (October, 1967) 205–217.

13. Fortune, *A Fortune Survey on Locating Plants, Warehouses, and Laboratories* (New York: Time, 1963).

14. Blair T. Bower, "The Location Decision of Industry and Its Relationship to Water," in *Economics in the Decision Making Process, Water Resources and the Economic Development of the West*, report No. 13 (San Francisco: Western Agricultural Economics Research Council, Committee on the Economics of Water Resource Development, 1964) p. 141.

15. See: William Cris Lewis, "An Econometric Model of Urban-Rural Structure and Growth," (unpublished Ph.D. thesis, Iowa State University, 1969).

16. This section is a brief summary of the concepts articulated in W. Cris Lewis, "Public Investment Impacts and Regional Economic Growth," *Water Resources Research*, August 1973.

17. See: Stanislow Czamanski, "A Model of Urban Growth," *Papers of the Regional Science Association*, XIII (1964) 177–200.
    Czamanski, "A Method of Forecasting Urban Growth by Distributed Lag Analysis", *Journal of Regional Science*, V, 1 (1965) 15–50.

18. Charles L. Leven, "Some Problems in Establishing a National Water Policy," (statement before the National Water Commission, Washington, D.C., November 5, 1970) p. 1.

19. See: Niles M. Hansen, "A Growth Center Strategy for the United States," *The Review of Regional Studies*, Vol. 1, No. 1, 161–173.
    Hansen, *Intermediate-Size Cities as Growth Centers: Applications for Kentucky, the Piedmont Crescent, the Ozarks*, and Texas (New York: Praeger Publishers, 1971).
    Gordon C. Cameron, "Growth Areas, Growth Centres, and Regional Conversion," *Scottish Journal of Political Economy*, XVII (February, 1970) 19–38.
    E.A.G. Robinson, (ed.), *Backward Areas in Advanced Countries* (New York: St. Martin's Press, 1969).

20. Hansen, "A Growth Center Strategy for the United States," p. 16.

7

A Review of Empirical Studies of Water Resource Investment and Economic Growth

To this point, the analysis has been primarily theoretical, with only a passing reference to any empirical evidence. To complement and support the theoretical arguments, several empirical studies of the relationship between water resources and their development and change in the level of regional economic activity will be reviewed in this chapter. None of these is sufficiently comprehensive, nor does any offer convincing quantitative evidence so as to be considered definitive. None would justify taking a position on the question of the relative efficacy of water investment as compared to other alternatives as a policy tool for promoting economic growth. In some, the basic research design was faulty; in others, the lack of a solid theoretical framework led to incomplete or otherwise misspecified functional relationships in the models used. Nevertheless, the findings are suggestive of certain developmental implications of water investment, and, for this reason, their review is considered to be worthwhile.

Howe,[1] in a widely noted paper, used analysis of variance techniques to determine if there were significant differences in the rate of economic growth[a] among regions (i.e., counties) classified with respect to water availability during the 1950~1960 period. Generally, the conclusions were negative. Regions without ample water resources, as measured by streamflow, availability of water transportation, and average annual runoff, were not characterized by below average growth, while regions well endowed with water were not guaranteed rapid growth. Howe's conclusion is probably a little strong, given that there were certain problems in his research design.

> While caution is required in drawing policy conclusions from the observations of this study, the evidence clearly indicates that water availability, including water transport, does not outweigh the other attributes possessed by regions which make them attractive or unattractive as the locus of different industries. It is clearly suggested that water resource developments are likely to be poor tools for accelerating regional economic growth if markets, factor availabilities, and other amenities of living are lacking.[2]

---

[a]The measures of economic growth used were percentage employment growth and percentage competitive shift, 1950~1960. The latter, from the "shift" or "shift-share" technique described in Chapter 3, is defined as the competitive shift as a percentage of the employment in 1950. It is designed as a measure of a region's relative input-output access. Water availability, if important to industry, should influence this measure, and its effect measurable by statistical techniques.

The conclusion does not follow directly from the analysis. Howe states that " . . . water resource developments are likely to be poor tools for accelerating regional economic growth . . . ," but he has really examined the relationship between water *availability* and growth, not *investment* and growth. It is possible that water availability did influence growth in many of these counties, but that the development impacts had been largely exhausted by 1950. Chicago, Illinois, is a case in point. Location on Lake Michigan and the Chicago River probably offered a great many advantages during the early development of the city and explained a significant part of the city's economic development. By 1950, however, most of these advantages had been captured, and the city actually experienced a population decline during the 1950-1960 decade. All of the population growth in the metropolitan area was in the suburbs, many of which are poorly endowed with water.

A more recent study by Cox, Grover, and Siskin [3] examined the growth implications of large multiple-purpose water projects in 61 counties during the 1948-1958 period. Although qualifying their conclusions because of the limited geographic scope of their observations, they found no statistically significant relationship between project size and regional growth.

> We concluded it is dubious whether water resource projects serve as a stimulus to economic growth for the strictly rural counties in the northeastern United States. We must seriously consider the possibility, as Howe did in his study of larger regions, that water resource developments are likely to be poor tools for accelerating economic growth of small rural regions of the northeastern United States.[4]

This conclusion is based on the fact that variables measuring the availability of water and water-related services were not selected out of a larger set of explanatory variables for inclusion in any of final regression equations specified by a stepwise technique.

There are some rather serious methodological problems here. For example, the relative contribution of any one variable to the ratio of explained mean square to unexplained or error mean square is conditional on the variables already in the equation. It is possible, in fact quite probable, given the large number of variables under consideration, that variables already in the equation were colinear with the water variables, and that the explanatory power of the latter has already been largely accounted for by the former. In such a situation, the addition of the water variable could hardly be expected to result in a significant increase in the equational statistics (F) and thus they would not be selected for inclusion Furthermore, as the data were drawn only on rural counties in one region, the conclusions could only be narrowly applied.

Garrison,[5] in a study of the Tennessee Valley area, concluded that water availability significantly influenced the microlocation (i.e., within region) of water-oriented employment. Significant positive relationships were found between employment levels, employment growth, and surplus employment (Garrison's term for the competitive shift) on the one hand, and water availability as measured by 7-day, 10-year minimum flows. Counties were placed into eleven different classes of water availability, which allowed the estimation of a threshold level of water availability at 400 cfs for the concentration of water-oriented employment.[b] The differential magnitude of the competitive shift among counties with varying water availability was quite dramatic. The shifts were overwhelmingly negative in the nonwater counties (those with streamflow less than 400 cfs) and consistently positive in the counties with relatively large water endowments.

While the data in the Garrison study are quite convincing, the analysis suffers from a problem that is just the reverse of that in the Cox, Grover, and Siskin study—a failure to estimate the relationship between water-oriented employment and a number of relevant explanatory variables, including water, in a multivariate framework. It would be more convincing to show a significant, positive relationship between water and employment when the influence of a number of other variables had been held constant. A simple regression equation probably is insufficient in attempting to explain a process as complex as regional growth.

Although his empirical estimates are somewhat contradictory, Ben-David [6] develops a sound theoretical model of water supply-demand relationships to derive a statistical test of the hypothesis that water accounts for a significant part of the total cost structure in some industries, and, therefore, plays an important role in the location decision of those industries. Data from counties in 14 states in the eastern half of the U.S. were used in a multiple regression analysis. Water-oriented employment was regressed on manufacturing wages, market potential, nonwater-oriented employment, and water availability, measured by low-flow miles in all stream segments of the county. Based primarily on the partial regression coefficients on the logarithm of water availability (0.169) Ben-David concludes:

> Water projects that will add to water availability of an area in which water is not abundant (by increasing the minimum low flows) will make the area more attractive to water-oriented industry, and we could expect an increase of 0.169 percent in employment for a one percent change in water availability.[7]

This conclusion is based on an equation estimated with data from all water-

---

[b]This possible existence of a threshold level of water availability for inducing employment growth constitutes another weakness of the Howe paper. His variables were set up so that any existing threshold might not be identified, and, if present, would be likely to render the water availability variable incapable of reflecting the true relationship.

oriented industries. Equations estimated for each of these five industries (at the 2-digit SIC level) yielded widely varying results, in both size and level of significance of regression coefficients. These coefficients and their associated t-values are: food and kindred products—0.039 (0.4); paper and allied products—0.301 (1.6); chemicals and allied products—0.049 (0.2); petroleum and coal products—-2.034 (-0.4); and primary metals—0.549 (3.33). Thus, only one coefficient is statistically significant,[c] one is negative, and only two are of approximately the same order of magnitude.

In summary, the empirical research on the subject is somewhat confusing. While there is some evidence of a positive relationship between water development and employment growth, particularly in water-intensive industries, the degree of the relationship, particularly at the individual industry level, is still unknown. This is not inconsistent with the theoretical findings of the earlier chapters, where water was found to be production input of secondary importance for some industries, and one for which there existed several sources of supply (e.g., recycling, self-supplied through wells, purchase of municipal water, etc.). These rather unique characteristics of the resource suggest that it might be difficult to use statistical tools to estimate the effects of increased supplies and/or quality.

Notes

1. Charles W. Howe, "Water and Regional Growth in the United States, 1950–1960," *Southern Economic Journal*, XXXIV, 4 (April, 1968) 477–499.
2. *Ibid.*, p. 488.
3. P. Thomas Cox, Wilfred Grover, and Bernard Siskin, "Effects of Water Resource Investment on Economic Growth," *Water Resources Research*, VII, 1 (February, 1971) 32–39.
4. *Ibid.*, p. 37.
5. Charles B. Garrison, *Effect of Water Resources on Economic Growth in the Tennessee Valley Region*, (Knoxville: University of Tennessee, Department of Economics, January, 1971).
6. Shaul Ben-David, "Effects of Water Development on Location of Water Oriented Manufacturing," in George S. Tolley, ed., *Estimation of First Round and Selected Subsequent Income Effects of Water Resource Investment*, U.S. Army Engineer Institute for Water Resources (Springfield, Virginia: Clearinghouse for Federal Scientific and Technical Information, February, 1970).
7. *Ibid.*, p. 78.

---

[c]Defined as being significantly different from zero at the 0.05 or lower probability level.

Part III
Measuring the Impacts of Water Development

The three chapters that constitute Part III are designed to demonstrate the application of the basic concepts and theories outlined in Parts I and II. In these chapters the basic theory is also extended. The goal is to bring together the various aspects of the argument presented thus far, and to demonstrate how these might be applied in the analysis or evaluation of any one of a range of investments in a particular type of region.

In Chapter 8 the concepts of regional delineation and measurement of economic growth are used to develop an accounting framework for analyzing the developmental impacts of each of an array of water resources investments. Consideration is given to classifying regions by their economic structure and stage of development and water resource investments by the economic services forthcoming directly from the project (i.e., water supply, power, recreation, etc.) The functional economic area (FEA) is used as the basic spatial unit.

A matrix format is used which includes a detailed project area impact matrix which accounts for all direct and indirect effects in each FEA of the project area; and a multiregion impact matrix which traces the economic effects to other regions that are linked to the project area. Measures for levels of economic activity, economic structure, welfare, and the environment are included.

Techniques for making quantitative estimations of these economic impacts are reviewed in Chapter 9. The empirical procedures of linear programming, input-output, simulation, and econometric modeling are discussed, and examples of their application in water-oriented problems are indicated. It is shown that no one technique or tool is the most useful in every application, and in some cases several techniques must be combined. The problem of data availability, procurement, and manipulation is also given brief mention.

Finally, in Chapter 10, several hypothetical case studies are analyzed. An assessment is made of the economic effects of various single-purpose water investments in three region types: an urban-industrial complex, an agricultural area, and an area where the economic structure is undergoing change from being heavily dependent on agriculture to a situation where manufacturing employment is becoming dominant.

8 An Accounting Framework for Public Water Investment Impacts

In this chapter a comprehensive framework is outlined which can be used to account for the economic impacts of water resource investments. Essentially, a system of matrices is developed which cross-classifies developmental or growth impacts by region and investment type. The matrix system might serve as a prototype in the development of a planner's handbook on water investment impact analysis. In Chapter 10, certain of the more interesting investment-region combinations will be analyzed in the form of a set of hypothetical case studies.

Two points are important. First, the effects of the investment are considered from a national perspective because of the possibility of regional offsets. To do this, impacts felt in the nonproject regions must be identified and measured. If the decision-maker's interests were more parochial, as might be the case in a state development agency or local chamber of commerce, this multiregional model might be discarded in favor of one focusing on a single region or project area. Second, both direct and indirect effects must be estimated. Using the standard input-output model definition, the direct effects are those caused by the initial reactions of both producers and consumers to the stream of services provided by the water project. These direct effects need not be limited to the project area. For example, the development of a recreation area in Region A may almost immediately reduce tourism in Region B. The indirect effects are those due to linkages of directly affected producers and consumers with other producers and consumers. Because of the highly interdependent economic system, initial effects in a few sectors will lead to multiple effects in many, if not all other sectors.[a] The dual goal of considering multiregional and direct-indirect impacts suggests that interregional input-output models would have significant utility in these analyses.

Clearly, development impacts in Region A will have indirect impacts in Region B, which will cause further repercussions in A. The interregional input-output model is ideally suited for the assessment of these effects, as the final solution yields output levels in all industries in all regions after all equilibrating output changes have been made. Indeed, much of the recent work in this area, including that by Leven,[1] Tolley,[2] Bargur,[3] and Davis,[4] depends heavily on such models.

---

[a]Ideally, the analysis could be extended to include the associated "induced" effects. These are defined as those changes in output following a change in final demand, the latter caused by the change in income associated with the direct and indirect effects.

To develop the comprehensive planning matrix, consider a national economy composed of m regions. In the limit these might be the 305 functional economic areas as defined by Berry,[5] augmented to exhaust the area of the country. These regions are then classified into p region types using a set of regional characteristics.

Table 8-1, the Comprehensive Water Investment Planning Matrix, shows developmental impacts cross-classified by investment and region type, with the investment type being further classified into the economic services (e.g., water supply, transportation, recreation, etc.) provided by that project. Each cell or entry of this matrix, M_{ij}^k, refers to two other more detailed matrices where the impacts of service k generated by investment type j in region i are analyzed in detail. Clearly, many of the M_{ij}^k will be zero, or sufficiently small that they would warrant little or no consideration.[b] Examples of the latter would include the provision of irrigation water to a completely urbanized area; while there might be some services provided, they would probably not have any perceptible influence on economic growth or development in the region. Zero entries would be found in the columns where that particular service is not provided by that type of investment. For example, some groundwater development projects are of the single purpose type and, therefore, entries under all other service columns would be zero.

The inclusion of an impact column for each service provided by a multiple-purpose project should not suggest that the possibility of development impacts associated with the interaction of the various services is ruled out. As suggested earlier, it is possible that the total impact of, say, a two-purpose investment would be greater than the sum of the impacts associated with each purpose, where the benefits were spatially isolated but in identical regions. At this stage, however, no effort is made to estimate these interactions or to make provisions for them in the impact matrix.

Each nonzero entry in this matrix would be uniquely associated with two additional impact matrices. The first, a Project Area Impact Matrix (Table 8-2), would include estimates of the direct and indirect impacts on all relevant measures for each FEA in the project area. The variables used to describe regional change would be categorized as measures useful in evaluating the project with respect to the three criteria established by the Water Resources Council, as discussed in Chapter 1.

Where such addition is appropriate (i.e., total income, population, employment, etc.), the impacts are summed across FEA's to allow evaluation for the entire project area. In general, additivity is limited to the measures of regional development. However, the matrix does provide for a very efficient way of

---

[b]If there are p region types, K water-oriented services, and J investment types, the matrix will have $p \cdot K \cdot J$ cells, but, as many of these combinations are of little or no interest, the number that would have to be analyzed in an actual applied situation is considerably smaller than $p \cdot K \cdot J$.

Table 8-1
Comprehensive Water Investment Planning Matrix

Region Type	Investment Type 1							Investment Type 2								Investment Type K						
	S	T	R	P	I	H	F	S	T	R	P	I	H	F	....	S	T	R	P	I	H	F
1	M_{11}^S	M_{11}^T	·	·	·	·	M_{11}^F	M_{12}^S	M_{12}^T	·	·	·	·	M_{12}^F		M_{1K}^S	M_{1K}^T	·	·	·	·	M_{1K}^F
2	M_{21}^S	·	·	·	·	·	M_{21}^F	M_{22}^S	·	·	·	·	·	M_{22}^F		M_{2K}^S	·	·	·	·	·	M_{2K}^F
·																						
·																						
·																						
P	M_{P1}^S	·	·	·	·	·	M_{P1}^F	M_{P2}^S	·	·	·	·	·	M_{P2}^F		M_{PK}^S	·	·	·	·	·	M_{PK}^F

Code for Project Services:

S — Municipal and industrial Supply
T — Transportation
R — Recreation
P — Pollution control
I — Irrigation
H — Hydroelectric power
F — Flood control

Table 8-2
Project Area Impact Matrix (M_{ij}^k)

	FEA 1		FEA 2		. . .	FEA m		Region = Σ FEA i	
	Direct	*Indirect*	*Direct*	*Indirect*		*Direct*	*Indirect*	*Direct*	*Indirect*
Regional Growth – National Efficiency									
Income									
Population									
Employment									
Agriculture									
Mining									
Manufacturing (W.I.)									
Other manufacturing									
Miscellaneous									
Social Well-Being									
% Urban									
% Manufacturing employment									
% Agricultural employment									
Per capita income									
Income distribution									
% < $3,000									
% $3,000 – $10,000									
% > $10,000									
Unemployment rate									
Environmental Quality									
Environment									
Air quality index									
Water quality index									
Congestion index									

examining changes in social well-being and environmental quality in each of the component FEA's. There will be changes in these measures for the entire project area that can be evaluated, but not computed as a sum over all FEA's.

As national economic efficiency is still an important criterion, it is necessary to measure impacts that might occur outside the project region. In Table 8–3, the Multi-Region Impact Matrix allows the recording of the socioeconomic effects on each region of the country. Because many projects will produce regional offsets, it is important to consider the national perspective.[c] Examples of such offsets would include the movement of a productive facility from one region to another, the shifting of tourists from one site to another, and the price effects that might result from the increased agricultural production following a large irrigation project.

Notes

1. Charles L. Leven, ed., *Development Benefits of Water Resource Investments*, a report submitted to the U.S. Army Corps of Engineers, Institute for Water Resources (Springfield, Virginia: Clearinghouse for Federal Scientific and Technical Information, November, 1969).
2. George S. Tolley, ed. *Estimation of First Round and Selected Subsequent Income Effects of Water Resources Investment*, a report submitted to the U.S. Army Corps of Engineers, Institute for Water Resources (Springfield, Virginia: Clearinghouse for Federal Scientific and Technical Information, February, 1970).
3. Jona Bargur, *Economic Evaluation of Water, Part VI: A Dynamic Inter-regional Input-Output Programming Model of the California and Western States Water Economy*, Water Resources Center Contribution No. 128 (Berkeley: Sanitation Engineering Research Laboratory, University of California, June, 1969).
4. H. Craig Davis, *Economic Evaluation of Water, Part V: Multiregional Input-Output Techniques and Western Water Resources Development*, Water Resources Center Contribution No. 125 (Berkeley: Sanitation Engineering Research Laboratory, University of California, February, 1968).
5. Brian J.L. Berry, Peter Goheen, and Harold Goldstein, *Metropolitan Area Definition: A Re-Evaluation of Concept and Practice*, working paper No. 28, U.S. Department of Commerce (Washington, D.C., 1968).

---

[c]This matrix would appear to be a particularly useful tool for computation of benefit-cost ratios.

Table 8-3
Multiregion Impact Matrix*

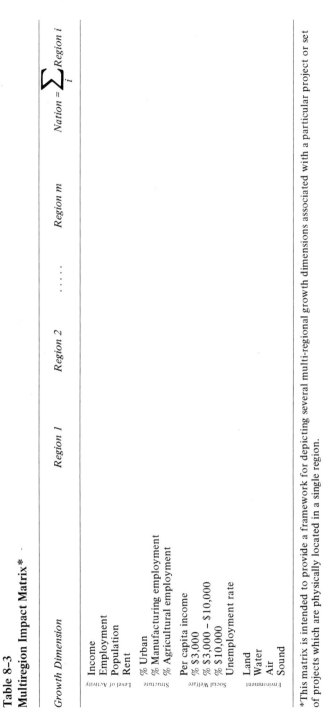

Growth Dimension		Region 1	Region 2	. . . . .	Region m	Nation $= \sum_i$ Region i
Level of Activity	Income					
	Employment					
	Population					
	Rent					
Structure	% Urban					
	% Manufacturing employment					
	% Agricultural employment					
Social Welfare	Per capita income					
	% $3,000					
	% $3,000 – $10,000					
	% $10,000					
	Unemployment rate					
Environment	Land					
	Water					
	Air					
	Sound					

*This matrix is intended to provide a framework for depicting several multi-regional growth dimensions associated with a particular project or set of projects which are physically located in a single region.

9

Quantitative Techniques for Economic Analysis of Water Resource Development

The application of the accounting framework outlined in the previous chapter will require the use of one or more of a set of quantitative tools to estimate or predict the various economic impacts. It is clear that no empirical technique offers a panacea for water resources evaluation and planning. Differing situations and analytical goals suggest the need for a range of quantitative tools. Econometric models, input-output analysis, optimization techniques, simulation studies, etc., all can play a role. For example, questions concerning the optimal use of water resources can often be answered by application of one of the several programming models available. Estimation of the quantitative relationship between water services and measures of economic change can be accomplished by econometric methods. Simulation provides a means for predicting the course of development of a regional economy under a variety of assumptions concerning water resources development. In some situations two or more techniques will have to be employed.

The purpose of this chapter is to briefly review several of the more widely used techniques to demonstrate their possible use in the analysis of water investments, and to note references to their applications. This discussion will be extended in Chapter 10, where several of these methods will be used in a set of hypothetical case studies of the effects of water resource development on a regional economy.

Input-Output Analysis

Input-output (I-O) analysis,[a] essentially an examination of the general equilibrium conditions of production, can serve at least four basic purposes. First, it can provide a detailed description of a national, regional, or multiregional economy, by identifying and quantifying the linkages among the various sectors of the economy and the sectoral source and origin of exports and imports. In multiregional models these linkages are estimated on an interregional as well as an intersectoral basis. Second, given a set of final or exogenous demands, total output in each industry and requirements for primary factors can be determined.

---

[a]The basic input-output framework is well known and need not be repeated here. Chenery and Clark,[1] Leontief,[2] and Isard,[3] among others, present rather comprehensive treatments of the subject.

Third, the effects of change in the final demand vector, arising in either the private or public sector, can be traced through the entire economy and changes in industry output predicted in detail. Fourth, possible or predicted changes in production technology or relative prices can be incorporated by changing the technical coefficients of production.

Clearly, I-O tools can be used to describe and evaluate changes in a regional economy that might occur as a result of making a water resource investment in that region. These predicted changes would take the form of changes in the vector of final demands, the addition of new activities (sectors) to the regional economy, and/or changes in the technical coefficients. Other applications include using I-O to project future sectoral output levels under alternative assumptions of final demand. In studies focusing on the water economy, such projections are used to forecast water consumption in future time periods.[4] To illustrate how future water consumption might be estimated from an I-O framework, consider the following example.

Given a vector of final demands, $Z(t)$, for each of n future years (i.e., $t = 1, \ldots, n$), projected output levels in each of the region's m industries, $Q(t)$, are given by

$$Q(t) = (I - A)^{-1} Z(t) \qquad\qquad (9\text{-}1)$$

where A is the standard matrix of technical coefficients and I is the identity matrix, appropriately dimensioned. From data on estimated water use by industry,[5] form an $(m \times m)$ diagonal matrix (w), where the diagonal elements are water use coefficients (w_j), water requirements per dollar of output for each industry. Total water use by each industry, $w_{0j}(t)$, is determined by

$$w_{0j}(t) = w \, Q \, (t) \qquad\qquad (9\text{-}2)$$

and total water use, $w_0(t)$, for each time period is given by

$$w_0(t) = K \cdot w_{0j}(t) = \sum_j w_{0j}(t) \qquad\qquad (9\text{-}3)$$

where K is an $(1 \times m)$ vector of ones.

In this case, it is assumed that both the technical coefficients of production (a_{ij}) and the water use coefficients are fixed. That is, there is an invariant set of water requirements for a given set of industry outputs. As has been argued previously, the idea that there is a set of water requirements rather than a set of water demand functions in incorrect, and is another manifestation of the "water is different" syndrome. In some of the so-called water-short areas, such as in the western United States, increased demand for water in excess of any increase in supply should lead to either higher prices, if administrative bodies are sensitive to the use of price as a rationing tool, or failure to satisfy some buyers' demands at the fixed price. In either event, water users will find their consumption patterns are not fixed by rigid requirements, but are subject to a variety of substitution possibilities for water. This model can be operated with any set of water coefficients desired to simulate changing water use patterns.[b]

Perhaps the most limiting factor in the application of I–O models is the data requirement, particularly for regional and multiregional models. Although available only with a lag of several years, national input-output tables are reasonably well developed, but often are of limited value to the regional analyst. Differences in industry structure between the region and the nation, and the greater importance of external trade linkages in subnational models suggest limited utility associated with the use of national tables in a regional context. As it is virtually impossible to estimate the input-output structure of a region from published data, most of the major regional models have either made adjustments in the national tables (see, for example, the California [6] and Oregon [7] models), or have conducted surveys to obtain the necessary primary data, as in the Colorado River Basin model.[8] While the latter method is not without some rather serious problems, it is, nevertheless, probably the best way to approach a regional model. The cost of such surveys can, however, be prohibitive.

Despite the limitations and qualifications, input-output analysis remains a powerful tool of economic analysis. Its widespread use in a variety of applications is evidence of this assertion. Perhaps its most useful characteristic is the ability to trace the changes in output of one sector through the system to determine ultimate changes in output for each of the other sectors, the natural result in a highly-interdependent economic system. This property makes input-output tools especially useful in estimating the differential effects of alternative public investments, including those directed at the development of water resources.

Although the science of input-output analysis is essentially positive in nature, it can be combined with optimization models, such as linear programming, where normative propositions are often evidenced by the form of the objective function, to form a very powerful analytical system. Such a construct seems very well suited for the solution of goal-oriented problems in regional analysis.

In an earlier discussion of the measurement of economic growth, the possibility of water investment influencing the stability of regional income and

---

[b]Although an extremely powerful tool, input-output models have certain limitations, and the value of the technique is constrained by some of the assumptions that are commonly made. These include the following: constant coefficients of production over time; homogeneous outputs—the possibility of joint products is implicitly assumed away; and horizontal supply functions for producers—firms react to increased demand by increasing output not by increasing the price.

product flows was discussed. It is possible that, because of the existence of low-cost water services, the structure of the regional economy might be changed significantly, as would be true if an industrial complex developed in what had been a predominantly agricultural area. In such a case both the discounted present value and variance of the regional income stream would probably be altered. An interesting question can be raised at this point. Does a change in economic structure, which increases both the present value of the stream of expected future income (both total and per capita) and the variance associated with that stream, represent an increase in regional welfare? It is clear that an increase in the present value of income, holding constant the variance of that income stream, would represent an increase in welfare. But would the residents prefer a lower but more stable income stream to one that fluctuated significantly, the result, possibly, of changes in the level of national economic activity?

In the following discussion, a method of estimating changes in regional income stability will be outlined. Elements of an aggregative income determination model (introduced earlier in Chapter 3) and a multiregional input-output model, will be combined in a sequential approach to the estimation of the elasticity of regional income, with respect to changes in exogenous or final demands which might follow a water resource investment. It will be shown that the interregional income determination model can be set up in a form that makes it very similar to the conventional I-O model, and that the parameters of the income determination model could be derived from the input-output model.

One of the key elements in identifying this elasticity will be an assessment of existing forward and backward industry linkages, and changes in those linkages, both within the project area and between the project area and neighboring regions. Water investment effects will be seen as altering the technical coefficients of production and also the vector of final demands. The technical coefficients will change if the investment alters the average productivity of some resources. The final demand vector will change because increased productivity will allow greater output from a given set of inputs, and there will be a spatial redistribution of final demands as productivity changes lead to spatial shifts in comparative advantage among industries. The I-O structure, as hypothesized, should be capable of generating marginal propensities to consume locally and to import for all regions under consideration. These estimates can be used in an aggregative interregional income determination model, to enable generalizations to be made concerning effects of changes taking place within one region, on activity in other regions, and the multiple feedback effects of such changes. This analysis should provide quantitative estimates of the local multipliers, which will include primary and secondary impacts, and the stability of the income stream in the regions under study. Of particular importance are changes in multipliers, levels of income, and the stability of that income stream under alternative structures and levels of exogenous demand.

Consider the simplest kind of regionalized Keynesian model for an economy having p regions,

$$Y_i = E_i + X_i - M_i, i = 1, \ldots, p \tag{9-4}$$

where Y_i is regional output or income in region i; E_i is expenditures on consumption, investment, and government; and X_i and M_i represent exports and imports respectively. Assume the following relations hold:

$$E_i = a + b\ Y_i \tag{9-5}$$

$$M_i = f + d\ Y_i \tag{9-6}$$

$$X_i = X_0 \tag{9-7}$$

Where b and d are the marginal propensities to spend domestically (MPC) and import (MPI) respectively. Now solving for income yields

$$Y_i = \frac{1}{1 - (b - d)} (a + f + X_0) \tag{9-8}$$

As a first approximation of cyclical stability, consider the elasticity of income with respect to a change in one source of exogenous demand, in this case exports.

$$\epsilon_{y,x} = \frac{\partial Y}{\partial X} \cdot \frac{X}{Y} \tag{9-9}$$

where

$$\frac{\partial Y}{\partial X} = \frac{1}{1 - (b - d)} \tag{9-10}$$

Substituting $X = Y - E + M$ rewriting (9-9) yields

$$\epsilon = \frac{1}{1 - (b - d)} \left(1 - \frac{M}{Y} - \frac{E}{Y}\right) \tag{9-11}$$

This simple model, although demonstrating the process of regional income fluctuations, is incomplete, as it does not give explicit consideration to interregional feedback effects. Recall the following Equation (3-15) from the discussion of growth models:

$$Y_i = \frac{S_i + \sum_j \mu_{ij} Y_j}{1 - (c_i - \sum_j \mu_{ij})}, i = 1, \ldots, p \tag{9-12}$$

where S_i is the sum of exogenous demands, the μ_{ij} are the marginal propensities to import, and c_i are the marginal propensities to consume. Now the export elasticity of income is given by

$$\epsilon_{y_i, x_i} = \frac{\partial Y_i}{\partial X_i} \cdot \frac{X_i}{Y_i} = \frac{1}{1 - (c_j - \sum_j \mu_{ij})} \cdot \frac{\sum_j \mu_{ij} Y_j}{Y_i} \tag{9-13}$$

But the level of Y_j is not independent of Y_i since

$$Y_j = \frac{S_j + \sum_i \mu_{ij} Y_i}{1 - (c_j - \sum_i \mu_{ij})} \tag{9-14}$$

so that it is impossible to determine income in any one region or the elasticity coefficient without determining in the equilibrium level in all regions.

Equation system (9–12), one function for each of the p regions under consideration, can be solved in the following way. Set

$$R_i = \frac{1}{1 - (c_i - \sum_j \mu_{ij})} \tag{9-15}$$

$$Y = \begin{bmatrix} Y_1 \\ Y_2 \\ \cdot \\ \cdot \\ \cdot \\ Y_p \end{bmatrix}, S = \begin{bmatrix} S_1/R_1 \\ S_2/R_2 \\ \cdot \\ \cdot \\ \cdot \\ S_p/R_p \end{bmatrix}, \Gamma = \begin{bmatrix} 0 & \mu_{12}/R_2 & \mu_{13}/R_3 & \cdots & \mu_{1p}/R_p \\ \mu_{21}/R_1 & 0 & \mu_{23}/R_3 & \cdots & \mu_{2p}/R_p \\ & & \cdot & & \\ & & \cdot & & \\ & & \cdot & & \\ \mu_{p1}/R_1 & \mu_{p2}/R_2 & \cdots & \cdots & 0 \end{bmatrix} \tag{9-16}$$

Now rewriting (9–11) as

$$Y = S + \Gamma Y \tag{9-17}$$

the system can be solved for the region income vector, Y, by

$$Y = (I_p - \Gamma)^{-1} S \qquad (9\text{-}18)$$

which is the reduced form of the structural system as described in either
(9-12) or (9-17). Each of the elements of the $(I - \Gamma)^{-1}$ matrix, γ_{ij}, may be
thought of as a multiplier relating a change in income in region i to a change in
exogenous demand in region j. Using system (9-18), the total (both direct and
indirect) change in income resulting from a change in a parameter or any
exogenous demand can be traced through the entire regional system. Primary
or first order impacts can be determined from (9-17) and secondary impacts by
subtracting primary from total impacts.

Within the framework of this model, the stability of region i is approxi-
mated by computing the elasticity of income with respect to a change in either
a parameter or an exogenous expenditure. Consider an increase in government
spending $(G_j' > G_j)$ in region j. Clearly, j may equal i, which occurs when the
change in spending originates in the region under study. Now

$$S_j' = a_j + \bar{I}_j + \bar{G}_j' > S_j = a_j + \bar{I}_j + \bar{G}_j \qquad (9\text{-}19)$$

so that income in region i will change by

$$\Delta Y_i = \gamma_{ij} \Delta \bar{G}_j = \gamma_{ij} \Delta S_j \qquad (9\text{-}20)$$

where γ_{ij} is element ij in the $(I - \Gamma)^{-1}$ matrix, so that the measure of elasticity is
given by

$$\epsilon_{ij} = \frac{\partial Y_i}{\partial S_j} \cdot \frac{S_j}{Y_i} = \gamma_{ij} \frac{S_j}{Y_i} \qquad (9\text{-}21)$$

The levels of S_j and Y_i needed for the computation may be either the average
before and after the change or the initial values.

There are several implications to be drawn from this analysis. The total
impacts on regional income are rather complicated functions of the entire set of
marginal propensities to consume (c_i) and to import (μ_{ij}). That is, with a
significant amount of interregional trade (i.e., few $\mu_{ij} = 0$), the elements of
$(I - \Gamma)^{-1}$ will be functions of many, if not all, the elements in the original Γ
matrix.

The stability of the income stream in a region will vary depending on the
source of the shock. Rather than having one elasticity measure for each region,
there will be p measures for each region (i.e., ϵ_{ij} $j = 1, \ldots, p$), one for each of
the regions, including the "own" elasticity, (ϵ_{ii}).

Quantitative estimates of regional sensitivity to income change require estimates of the relative magnitude of the several parameters of the system. For operational use in a policy model, definitive point estimates of these parameters are required. It is at this point that an interregional input-output model can be of significant value. The μ_{ij} in the above are, by definition, weighted averages of certain technical coefficients in the multiregional I-O table—those that relate to interregional transactions.

In the following section, an interregional input-output model will be described and its application in estimating income multipliers and impact elasticities will be indicated. This type of model is useful in a water resources development context because it can provide detailed estimates of the economic effects of the investment, as well as allowing a comprehensive description of the changes in economic structure and flows that follow the project.

In Table 9-1 the basic structure of an interregional I-O system is presented. Beginning with the interregional transactions matrix for n industries in p regions[c]

$$Q = \begin{bmatrix} Q^{11} & Q^{12} & \cdots & Q^{1p} \\ Q^{21} & Q^{22} & \cdots & Q^{2p} \\ \cdot & & & \\ \cdot & & & \\ \cdot & & & \\ Q^{p1} & Q^{p2} & \cdots & Q^{pp} \end{bmatrix} \qquad (9\text{-}22)$$

where each Q^{KL} is an $(n \times n)$ matrix of interindustry transactions between regions K and L; that is

$$Q^{KL} = ||q_{ij}^{KL}||, (i, j = 1, \ldots, n) = \begin{bmatrix} q_{11}^{KL} & q_{12}^{KL} & \cdots & q_{1n}^{KL} \\ q_{21}^{KL} & q_{22}^{KL} & \cdots & q_{2n}^{KL} \\ \cdot & & & \\ \cdot & & & \\ \cdot & & & \\ q_{n1}^{KL} & q_{n2}^{KL} & \cdots & q_{nn}^{KL} \end{bmatrix} \qquad (9\text{-}23)$$

Compute a matrix (A) of technical coefficients (a_{ij}^{KL}), each denoting the dollar

---

[c]Lowercase subscripts index interindustry flows while uppercase superscripts index interregional flows.

input from industry i in region K per dollar of output of industry j in region L

$$A = || a_{ij}^{KL} || = \frac{q_{ij}^{KL}}{\sum_{i=1}^{n} q_{ij}^{L}} \; ; i, j = 1, \ldots, n; K, L = 1, \ldots, p \qquad (9\text{-}24)$$

A set of value added coefficients are given by

$$v_i^K = \frac{V_i^K}{Q_i^K} \; ; i = 1, \ldots, n; K = 1, \ldots, p \qquad (9\text{-}25)$$

The model is completed with the addition of a matrix of final demands

$$Z = \begin{bmatrix} Z^{11} Z^{12} & \cdots & Z^{1p} \\ Z^{21} Z^{22} & \cdots & Z^{2p} \\ \cdot & & \\ \cdot & & \\ \cdot & & \\ Z^{p1} Z^{p2} & \cdots & Z^{pp} \end{bmatrix} \qquad (9\text{-}26)$$

where each Z^{KL} is an $(n \times 1)$ vector of final demands arising in region L for output produced in region K, and a vector of industry outputs,

$$Q = \begin{bmatrix} Q^1 \\ Q^2 \\ \cdot \\ \cdot \\ \cdot \\ Q^p \end{bmatrix} \qquad (9\text{-}27)$$

where each Q^K is an $(n \times 1)$ vector of industry outputs in region K. Output is equal to intermediate plus final demands:

$$Q = A Q + Z U \qquad (9\text{-}28)$$

Table 9-1
Structure of an Interregional Input-Output System

| | | | Region | | | | | | | | | | | | | Final Demand* | | |
| | | 1 | | | 2 | | | | ⋯ | | p | | | | | Demanding Region | | |
Producing Sector	Consuming Sector	1	2	⋯	n	1	2	⋯	n	⋯	1	2	⋯	n		1	2	⋯	p
Region 1 1		a^{11}_{11}	a^{11}_{12}	⋯	a^{11}_{1n}	a^{12}_{11}		⋯	a^{12}_{1n}	⋯	a^{1p}_{11}		⋯	a^{1p}_{1n}		Z^{11}_{1}	Z^{12}_{1}	⋯	Z^{1p}_{1}
2		a^{11}_{21}	a^{11}_{22}	⋯	a^{11}_{2n}											Z^{11}_{2}	Z^{12}_{2}	⋯	Z^{1p}_{2}
⋮																			
n		a^{11}_{n1}	⋯	⋯	a^{11}_{nn}	a^{21}_{n1}	⋯	⋯	a^{21}_{nn}	⋯	a^{1p}_{n1}	⋯	⋯	a^{1p}_{nn}		Z^{11}_{n}	Z^{12}_{n}	⋯	Z^{1p}_{n}
Region 2 1		a^{21}_{11}	⋯	⋯	a^{21}_{1n}	a^{22}_{11}	⋯	⋯	a^{22}_{1n}	⋯	a^{2p}_{11}	⋯	⋯	a^{2p}_{1n}		Z^{21}_{1}	Z^{22}_{1}	⋯	Z^{2p}_{1}
⋮																			
n		a^{21}_{n1}	⋯	⋯	a^{21}_{nn}	a^{22}_{n1}	⋯	⋯	a^{22}_{nn}	⋯	a^{2p}_{n1}	⋯	⋯	a^{2p}_{nn}		Z^{21}_{n}	Z^{22}_{n}	⋯	Z^{2p}_{n}
⋮																			
Region p 1		a^{p1}_{11}	⋯	⋯	a^{p1}_{1n}	a^{p2}_{11}	⋯	⋯	a^{p2}_{1n}	⋯	a^{pp}_{11}	⋯	⋯	a^{pp}_{1n}		Z^{p1}_{1}	Z^{p2}_{1}	⋯	Z^{pp}_{1}

	1	2	...	n	1	2	...	n	...	1	...	n	Q^p	Z_n^{p1}	Z_n^{p2}	...	Z_n^{pp}
p																	
⋮																	
n	a_{n1}^{p1}	...		a_{nn}^{p1}	a_{n1}^{p2}	...		a_{nn}^{p2}	...	a_{n1}^{pp}	...	a_{nn}^{pp}	Q_1^p	Z_n^{p1}	Z_n^{p2}	...	Z_n^{pp}
Value added	v_1^1 v_2^1	...		v_n^1	v_1^2	...		v_n^2	...	v_1^p	...	v_n^p	v_1^p	v_n^p	v_f^1	v_f^2	...	v_f^p
Total output	Q_1^1 Q_2^1	...		Q_n^1	Q_1^2	...		Q_n^2	...	Q_1^p	...	Q_n^p	Q_1^p					

*Z_i^{KL} is final demand for output of industry i in region K originating in region L. $\bar{Z}$, a column of total final demands for each industry in each region, is derived by $\bar{Z}_{(n \times 1)}^K = Z_{(n \times n)}^K U_{(n \times 1)}$ where U is a vector of ones.

where U is a $(p \times 1)$ unit vector. Solving for Q yields output of each industry in each region conditional on the given set of final demands:

$$Q = (I - A)^{-1} (Z U) \tag{9-29}$$

Defining the elements of the $(I - A)^{-1}$ matrix as γ_{ij}^{KL}, output of the ith sector and K^{th} region is given by

$$Q_i^K = \left[\sum_{L=1}^{p} \sum_{j=1}^{n} \gamma_{ij}^{KL} \left(\sum_{K=1}^{p} Z_i^{KL} \right) \right] \tag{9-30}$$

Thus the γ_{ij}^{KL}'s are the impact multipliers for output,

$$\partial X_i^K / \partial Z_j^L = \gamma_{ij}^{KL} \tag{9-31}$$

Output elasticities are given by

$$\epsilon_{ij}^{KL} = \partial X_i^K / \partial Z_j^L \cdot \frac{Z_j^L}{X_i^K} = \gamma_{ij}^{KL} (Z_j^L / X_i^K) \tag{9-32}$$

but

$$X_i^K = \sum_{L=1}^{p} \sum_{j=1}^{n} \gamma_{ij}^{KL} Z_j^L \tag{9-33}$$

so the elasticity reduces to

$$\epsilon_{ij}^{KL} = \left(\gamma_{ij}^{KL} / \sum_{L=1}^{p} \sum_{j=1}^{n} \gamma_{ij}^{KL} \right) \tag{9-34}$$

There will be $n^2 p^2$ elasticities, one for each industry-region combination relative to each industry-region source of final demand. Note that this I-O analysis is analogous to that described in the previous section on income determination models, but the difference in data requirements and information generated for the two models is huge.

Assume that regions are closed with respect to purchase of primary factors (i.e., labor); the direct impact of changes in output in region one will offset value added in that region only. Also assume regional income to be proportional to value added,

$$Y^K = \alpha^K V^K \qquad (9\text{-}35)$$

Value added multipliers are found by

$$\partial V^K / \partial Z_i^L = \sum_{i=1}^{n} (\partial V^K / \partial X_i^K \cdot \partial X_i^K / \partial Z_j^L) \qquad (9\text{-}36)$$

which reduces to

$$\partial V^K / \partial Z_j^L = \sum_{i=1}^{n} (v_i^K \cdot \gamma_{ij}^{KL}) \qquad (9\text{-}37)$$

Regional income multipliers are determined in the following way:

$$(\partial Y_K / \partial V^K \cdot \partial V^K / \partial Z_j^L) = \alpha^K \frac{\partial V^K}{\partial Z_j^L} = \alpha^K \cdot \sum_{i=1}^{n} (v_i^K \cdot \gamma_{ij}^{KL}) \qquad (9\text{-}38)$$

Finally, value added and regional income elasticities are indicated by the following functions:

$$\epsilon_{V^K, Z_j^L} = \sum_{i=1}^{n} (v_i^K \cdot \gamma_{ij}^{KL}) \cdot \frac{Z_j^L}{\displaystyle\sum_{j=1}^{n} v_j^K Q_j^K} \qquad (9\text{-}39)$$

and

$$\epsilon_{Y^K, Z_j^L} = \alpha^K \cdot \sum_{i=1}^{n} (v_i^K \gamma_{ij}^K) \cdot \frac{Z_j^L}{\alpha^K \cdot (\epsilon v_j^K \cdot Q_j^K} = \epsilon_{V^K, Z_j^L} \qquad (9\text{-}40)$$

The income impact elasticity reduces to the value added impact elasticity because of the proportionality between the two variables.

Programming Models in Public
Investment Analysis

Programming models are designed to show the way to exploit a set of resources and related parameters in order to optimize (i.e., maximize or minimize) a given objective stated as a mathematical function.[9] The use of such models in economics usually involves the programming of a set of diverse activities so as to maximize profit or output, or minimize cost, given a set of resources, technology (in the form of production coefficients), and a set of prices for both outputs and inputs. The following types of questions lend themselves to programming analysis at least conceptually, if not empirically.[d] How can an underdeveloped region best exploit limited supplies of capital and skilled labor in order to maximize gross regional product? How should limited water supplies be allocated among sectors, particularly between agriculture and manufacturing, in order to maximize the value of output? Thus, programming models, in contrast with intput-output models, provide guidelines for normative economic policy in the sense of offering answers to questions such as how to combine resources, what level of production of various commodities to produce, and what are the values of incremental units of the resources applied, if resources are efficiently used.

For water resources research, programming models are primarily useful in two ways. First, the primal solutions of such models are useful in predicting the impacts on total output, the spatial distribution of that output among production sites, interregional commodity movements, and production costs associated with changes in resource availability and costs. For example, the economic effects of increasing water supply, reducing water cost, and/or lowering transportation costs (through navigable waterway construction) can be estimated by comparing the solutions to an appropriate programming model before and after the change. Second, the dual solution of programming models generates shadow prices for those resources used in the production process. These prices are often used in assigning values to those resources that are not traded in a competitive market (e.g., water). Essentially, the shadow price is theoretically equal to the price that would be determined for that resource under perfectly competitive conditions.

Although both the primal and dual types of estimates are forthcoming from

---

[d]Linear programming is not without its limitations. The use of linear objective functions and constraints may be unrealistic. However, this problem can be overcome through recourse to nonlinear programming techniques. In the linear models, there are also the problems of nondifferentiability and nonconvexity. In the first case, the solution to a linear program always occurs at one of the intersections of the linear constraints. Obviously, the severity of any problem introduced by this phenomenon will vary depending upon the degree of convexity and the number of active constraints. Such solutions imply that the technique is only discretely sensitive to changes in price parameters. In the second case, convexity of the "opportunity surface" is required to obtain a unique solution. Nonconvexity will result in a range of indifferent or multiple nonunique solutions.

the same programming model, each will be examined separately here. First, a rather comprehensive linear programming model is reviewed. If made operational, this model would be highly useful in predicting in detail the impacts of water resource investments, especially transportation. Then an assessment is made of two applied models where the primary purpose was to measure the value of water to certain sectors of a regional economy. A discussion of certain problems associated with programming techniques and a general statement on their efficacy in regional economic analysis completes this section of this chapter.

Leven and Read [10] outline a general linear programming framework for predicting the impact of changes in production costs, transportation costs, primary factor supplies, and demand for outputs on production costs and output at each of a set of production sites, shipments of goods among regions, and total production and transportation costs.

Assume the following variables:

$_i c_R$ = cost of all intermediate goods required to produce one unit of good R in region i ($i = 1, \ldots, I; R = 1, \ldots, K$)

$_i b_{rR}$ = quantity of primary good r required to produce one unit of good R in region i ($i = 1, \ldots, I; r = 1, \ldots, R; R = 1, \ldots, D$)

$_i R_R$ = unit value imputed to the physical capacity for the production of good R in region i

$_i W_r$ = imputed unit value of the endowment of primary good r in region i

$_i A_R$ = capacity for the production of good R in region i

$_j B_R$ = total demand for good R in region j ($j = 1, \ldots, J; R = 1, \ldots, K$)

$_i L_R$ = supply of primary good r available in region i^e

$_i e_r$ = unit price of primary good r in region i

$_{ij} S_R$ = cost of transporting one unit of good R from region i to region j

$_{ij} X_R$ = total quantity of good R produced in region i and shipped to region j

---

^{e}It is assumed that the supply functions for both primary factors and intermediate goods are perfectly elastic. The primary factors are limited in availability such that a point is reached where the supply function becomes perfectly inelastic.

$_{ij}Q$ = transportation capacity of the link between regions i and j

$_{ij}Y$ = imputed quasirent to one unit of capacity ($_{ij}Q$)

the program will determine the output in each region and the distribution of that output among regions ($_{ij}X_R$) that will minimize the sum of production and transport costs while satisfying demand requirements and supply limitations.

Thus, minimize

$$C = \sum_i \sum_j \sum_R \left\{ (_{ij}S_R) + \left[\sum_r (_ie_r)(_ib_{rR}) \right] + (_ic_R) \right\} (_{ij}X_R) \qquad (9\text{-}41)$$

(i.e., the total cost of producing and transporting all commodities in all regions is equal to the sum of per unit primary production, intermediate production, and transport costs, multiplied by the quantity of that good shipped to each region), subject to

$$\sum_i {}_{ij}X_R \geqslant {}_jB_R \ (j = 1, \ldots, J; R = 1, \ldots, k) \qquad (9\text{-}42)$$

(i.e., the amount of each good shipped must be sufficient to satisfy total demand in that region);

$$\sum_j {}_{ij}X_R \leqslant {}_iA_R \ (i = 1, \ldots, I; R = 1, \ldots, k) \qquad (9\text{-}43)$$

(i.e., production in region i must not exceed that region's capacity to produce it);

$$\sum_R \sum_j [{}_ib_{rR}] [{}_{ij}X_R] \leqslant {}_iL_R \ (i = 1, \ldots, I; r = 1, \ldots, R) \qquad (9\text{-}44)$$

(i.e., there is a capacity constraint on each region's supply of primary factors);

$$\sum_R {}_{ij}X_R \leqslant {}_{ij}Q \ (i = 1, \ldots, I; j = 1, \ldots, J) \qquad (9\text{-}45)$$

(i.e., the quantity of output shipped between any two regions cannot exceed the capacity of the transport link);

$$_{ij}X_R \geqslant 0 \text{ for all } i, j, \text{ and } R \qquad (9\text{-}46)$$

(i.e., no output can be negative).

The solution of the program (i.e., the determination of an optimal set of $_{ij}X_R$) defines output levels at each production site, the allocation of those outputs among the regional markets, the volume of shipments along each segment of the transportation network, and the total cost of such production and transportation. For purposes of this study, the impacts associated with a water resource investment would be measured by comparing solutions to the program before and after the investment. Water supply creating investment would change the supply of primary goods ($_iL_r$) in the project area, and, if the project lowered the price of water, there would also be a reduction in unit price of this primary good ($_ie_r$).[f] If water is viewed as an indirect input, rather than a primary good, expansion of water supplies may raise the ceiling on production or the production capacity variable ($_iA_R$).

The creation of a navigable waterway would probably increase the transportation capacities ($_{ij}Q$) of those parts of the transport network that can use the waterway and decrease the transportation cost ($_{ij}S_R$) on some products (those suitable for water transportation) shipped via these network segments.

The program just outlined is known as the primal problem, which deals with the physical quantities of outputs and inputs. Associated with every primal problem there is a dual problem which imputes values, or "shadow prices," to resources used in the production process.[g] The dual problem is: maximize

$$M = \sum_j \sum_R (_iP_R)(_jB_R) - \sum_i \sum_R (_iR_R)(_iA_R) - \sum_i \sum_r (_iW_r)(_iL_R)$$
$$- \sum_i \sum_j (_{ij}Q)(_{ij}Y) \qquad (9\text{-}47)$$

subject to

$$_jP_R - {}_iR_R - \sum_r (_iW_R)(_ib_{rR}) - (_{ij}Y) \leqslant {}_{ij}S_R + \sum_r (_ib_{rR})(_ie_r) + {}_ic_r$$
$$(i = 1, \ldots, I; J = 1, \ldots, J; R = 1, \ldots, k) \qquad (9\text{-}48)$$

---

[f] It is interesting that Leven and Read are somewhat dubious about the impact importance of changes in either water or power costs. Note the last sentence of this statement:[11]

> If we were interested in the impact of reduced water or electric power cost, however, the production function information that would be needed would be more complex. In particular, we would have to know both the average and marginal product of water and electricity in the production of the various commodities concerned. This would involve extremely difficult research, and so, accordingly, unless one had reason to believe that the impacts of increased water or electricity supply on industrial location would be significant, one should be very hesitant about engaging in the very difficult research that would be needed to estimate this impact.

[g] The constraints can be parametrically varied so that the dual problem produces a schedule relating the resource constraint and the shadow price, thus defining a demand function for that resource. This procedure overcomes the deficiencies inherent in the "requirements" approach or the single-valued estimate of "need" for water.

$$_jP_R \geq 0, \, _iW_r \geq 0, \, _iR_R \geq 0, \, _{ij}Y \geq 0 \text{ for all } i, j, R, \text{ and } r \qquad (9\text{-}49)$$

The solution to the dual problem yields the equilibrium or profit maximizing price for output ($_jP_R$) and shadow prices for physical production capacities ($_iA_R$), primary goods ($_iL_r$), which would include water supply, and transportation capacity ($_{ij}Q$).

An example of applied linear programming is the Lofting and McGauhey study of the California water economy.[12] They combined regional input-output and linear programming analyses to estimate and project the shadow price of water under alternative conditions for selected years from 1958 to 1990. Their model is simpler than that outlined by Leven and Read, as it focuses almost entirely on water supply and value in one region. Water is assumed to be the only basic resource constraining regional value added.

The model is formulated as follows: maximize

$$Y = V'Q \qquad (9\text{-}50)$$

subject to

$$W'Q \leq W_0 \qquad (9\text{-}51)$$

$$(I - A)Q \geq Z \qquad (9\text{-}52)$$

$$Q \geq 0 \qquad (9\text{-}53)$$

where

Y = regional value added

V = a vector of sectoral value added coefficients (v_j), the value in sector j per dollar of output

Q = a vector of gross output (Q_j) of each vector

W = a vector of sectoral water input coefficients (w_j), the water input required per dollar of output in sector j.

I = an identity matrix

A = a matrix of technical coefficients (a_{ij})

Z = a vector of sectoral final demands

W_0 = total fresh water withdrawal availability

Essentially the problem is to find that Q vector, the outputs of each of the region's industries, which will maximize regional value added ($V'Q$), subject to the constraint (9-51) that industry water requirements must be no greater than the available supplies, and (9-52) total output must be at least as great as final demand. Equation (9-53) represents a set of nonnegativity requirements for industry output.

Lofting and McGauhey developed estimates of the data and parameters necessary for empirically testing the model (i.e., the vectors of water coefficients (W) and projected final demands (Z), total water supply (W_0), and the technical coefficients matrix (A)). The program was solved under alternative assumptions of water supply availability. Roughly 43 million acre-feet were required for a feasible solution. That is, this quantity of water is the minimum necessary to meet specified levels of final demand. For this constraint, regional value added was $90.6 billion. The water constraint was gradually eased until at 79 million acre-feet this resource became redundant; value added at this level of water supply reaches its theoretical maximum of $139 billion.

The authors' estimate of the "safe yield" of water at 51.8 million acre-feet (1965) suggests that water is, in fact, a scarce resource, and, therefore, has a positive shadow price. The dual solution of the problem outlined above yielded the following relationship between shadow price and water constraint.

Fresh Water Withdrawal Constraint (000 acre-feet)	Shadow Price (1959 dollars per acre foot)
42,997–43,213	11,260
43,257–48,368	5,710
49,076–51,508	1,160
51,508–51,823	790
51,901–66,690	450
66,650–78,896	150

They conclude: [13]

> It can be noted that for the specified bill of final demands the model holds reasonably well when there are adequate supplies of water. As the water constraint is tightened, only the most "profitable" activities compete for it and an inordinately high value is imputed to it. This, nevertheless, demonstrates in a striking way the value of water under the truly competitive conditions of classical theory when there is a relative scarcity of the resource in question.

Econometric Models

An econometric model generally takes the form of a system of simultaneous equations which are descriptive of the structure and workings of a particular economy. The better known econometric models, including those developed by the University of Michigan,[14] Office of Business Economics,[15] and the Wharton School,[16] represent the entire national economy, but other models have been built for states, multicounty regions, cities, and industries, such as those developed by Bell [17] and Burton and Dyckman.[18] Econometric systems are useful in analyzing and explaining the structure of the economy under study, testing hypotheses about particular relationships, forecasting and simulating future economic change, and predicting the economic impact of change in specific exogenous variables, including the quality and availability of the several types of water resources.

The development of econometric models generally proceeds in four phases: specifications, estimation, testing, and application. In the specification stage, the relevant variables are combined in functional form, based on economic theory, a priori knowledge or conceptions of important relationships, or, possibly, through analysis of certain statistical relationships among variables. The parameters of the specified functions ordinarily are estimated by some type of regression technique, such as ordinary least squares or two- or three-stage least squares.[19] Other estimation techniques involve the use of linear and nonlinear programming methods.[20] The testing phase would include making significance tests for each parameter estimate and for such equational statistics as R^2, the ratio of explained to total variation in the dependent variables, and F, the ratio of mean square due to regression to mean square deviation from regression. Other tests involve the computation of predicted values of the dependent variables over a historic time period, and comparison of these values to the actual values during that interval. Theil's Inequality U coefficient is widely used in this type of comparison.[21] Application of the model includes its use to test hypotheses and to forecast or simulate the economy under alternative assumptions concerning levels of exogenous or predetermined variables.

The following paragraphs discuss the role of econometric models in the theory of economic policy, the basic structure of the typical econometric model, and a hypothetical model designed to measure the role and importance of water resources and investments therein in a regional economy.

In The *Theory of Economic Policy*,[22] Tinbergen outlines a framework for analyzing the basic interrelationships in the economic system, with particular reference to the way in which certain objectives might be attained. In Figure 9-1 this system is depicted graphically. Essentially, Tinbergen's policy model, which would probably take the form of a multiequation econometric model, combines a set of policy instruments, data or noncontrollable factors, and goals or target variables, in a way such that alternative levels of the policy variables can be related to levels of the target variables, and the latter then evaluated in terms of an objective or welfare function for society. The basic

Figure 9-1. The Theory of Economic Policy*

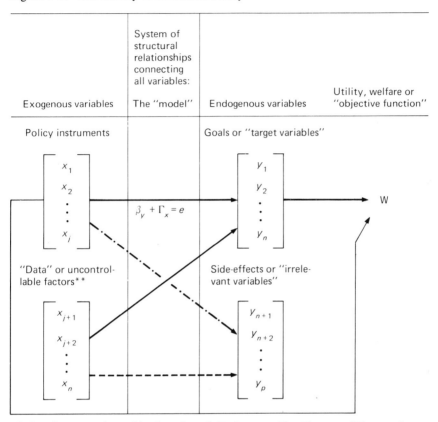

*Classification of variables based on **J. Tinbergen,** *The Theory of Economic Policy* (57)

**Not subject to control by the policy-maker or level of government that sets the goals and uses the policy instruments in question.

problem is one of selecting those values for the policy variables (which are constrained to lie within some predefined feasible set) that will maximize the social welfare function, given the levels of the noncontrollable factors.

Examples of the type of variables in each category would include the following:

Policy Instruments	Noncontrollable Factors	Target Variables
Tax rates	Weather	Income
Interest rates	Private investment	Output
Government spending	Consumer tastes	Employment
Money supply		Price level

The side-effect variables shown in Figure 9–1 include those things that are influenced by the level of economic activity but considered to be irrelevant or more amenable to control through means other than those associated with economic policy. For example, there tends to be a positive correlation between the unemployment rate and the frequency of certain types of crime (e.g., burglary, shoplifting, etc.). While crime is hardly irrelevant, it is probably best controlled by other than economic policy tools. Ten or fifteen years ago the effect of changes in economic activity on the environment might have been considered as irrelevant. Today, it is unlikely that any comprehensive model would exclude environmental impacts, even if these were considered only peripherally.

The Tinbergen framework is, perhaps, most easily made operational in a multiequation representation of the economic system. The econometric models developed for the United States can all be broken down into the components suggested in the Tinbergen framework. All are especially useful in estimating the differential impact of alternative public policies, which is measured by entering differential values for specific policy variables and then simulating the economic system over a number of time periods. The least operational element of this policy system is the social welfare function, which, by its very nature, defies specification, much less quantitative estimation. For "real world" application of the Theory of Economic Policy, the economist must depend on the collective judgment of political leaders in both the executive and legislative branches to provide him with the approximate weight to be given each target variable. Thus, the problem of estimating the social welfare function, at present, is more a political than an economic problem.

The basic structure of an econometric model is actually quite simple. Given a vector of the jointly dependent variables (y) and predetermined variables (x),[h]

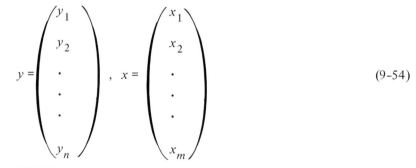

$$y = \begin{pmatrix} y_1 \\ y_2 \\ \cdot \\ \cdot \\ \cdot \\ y_n \end{pmatrix} , \quad x = \begin{pmatrix} x_1 \\ x_2 \\ \cdot \\ \cdot \\ \cdot \\ x_m \end{pmatrix} \qquad (9\text{-}54)$$

---

[h]Jointly dependent refers to those variables that will be determined by solving the system of equations. Predetermined refers to variables whose values are specified prior to solving the system. The terms jointly dependent and predetermined are roughly equivalent to the more common terms endogenous and exogenous, respectively. The former terms are somewhat more precise in meaning, and are preferred. For example, in a time-series model, a lagged endogenous variable is defined to be exogenous, although its value has not been determined outside the model. Predetermined variables would include those that are truly exogenous, as well as lagged endogenous variables.

and matrices of coefficients on the variables in each of these vectors (B and Γ),

$$
B = \begin{bmatrix} b_{11} \, b_{12} & \cdots & b_{1n} \\ b_{21} \, b_{22} & \cdots & b_{2n} \\ \cdot & & \\ \cdot & & \\ \cdot & & \\ b_{n1} & \cdots & b_{nn} \end{bmatrix}, \Gamma = \begin{bmatrix} \gamma_{11} \, \gamma_{12} & \cdots & \gamma_{1m} \\ \gamma_{21} \, \gamma_{22} & \cdots & \gamma_{2m} \\ \cdot & & \\ \cdot & & \\ \gamma_{n1} & \cdots & \gamma_{nm} \end{bmatrix} \qquad (9\text{-}55)
$$

the structural system of equations can be written as

$$ B\,x = \Gamma_y + e \qquad (9\text{-}56) $$

where e is a vector of random error terms. The reduced form of the structural system (9-56) is given by

$$ y = B^{-1}\,\Gamma\,X + B^{-1}\,e \qquad (9\text{-}57) $$

Each reduced form equation has only one jointly dependent variable as a function of predetermined variables only. As such, the reduced form is useful for assessing the total effect of an exogenous change, such as in the level of government investment, on particular endogenous variables. If there is simultaneity in the structural system, it is difficult to assess the total impact of an exogenous shock, because such a shock sets off a series of changes in all jointly dependent variables. Such changes are difficult to trace through the structural system.

To indicate an application of this structure, a simple multiequation model is formulated which is designated to estimate and predict the probable impacts that various types of water resources might have on regional economic growth, the latter to be measured by change in employment and population. The spatial-temporal dimensions of the model can be set up in one of two ways. The system might be representative of one region, composed, possibly, of one or several functional economic areas, and the parameters of the system estimated from time-series data. Alternatively, a cross-section model, representative of a typical, rather than a specific region, would be estimated from data gathered from a number of different regions for the same time period. The system to be outlined below will be structured as a cross-section model, bearing in mind that it could have been done either way, depending on the purposes to be served and data availability.[i]

---

[i]Because of the paucity of time-series data for many regions of the country, particularly the nonmetropolitan areas, and the need for a number of observations to generate reasonable statistical estimates of the parameters, it is likely that the actual development of this model would, of necessity, be based on cross-section data.

The model consists of five simultaneous equations, four behavioral relations, and one identity, in five jointly dependent and seven predetermined variables. These variables are defined in the following listing:

Jointly Dependent Variables

E_a = change in agricultural employment, 1960–1970

E_m = change in manufacturing employment, 1960–1970

E_r = change in residentiary employment, 1960–1970[j]

E = change in total employment, 1960–1970

P = change in population, 1960–1970

Predetermined Variables

W_{na} = nonagricultural wage rate in region, 1960

R = average annual rainfall in region

D = distance to nearest metropolitan area

WT = water transportation dummy = 1, if region is served by water transport; 0 otherwise

WS_I = an index of the cost and availability of irrigation water for the agriculture

WS_{MI} = an index of the cost, availability, and quality of water for municipal and industrial purposes

WR = an index measuring the size of, quality of, and ease of access to the region's water-based recreation resources

The classification of these predetermined variables as policy instruments or noncontrollable factors would depend on the purposes for which the model was intended. While average annual rainfall and distance to the nearest metro-

---

[j]Residentiary employment is defined to include that in the following sectors: retail, wholesale, services, public utilities, local government, etc.

politan area would seem to be unlikely policy instruments, each may be subject to some manipulation. For instance, rainfall might be varied by cloud-seeding activities; and distance, thought of as the time required to traverse the space, can be changed through investment in highways, airports, and other transport capital. As water and resource investment is of primary interest, consider variables W_{na}, R, and D as noncontrollable factors, and WT, WS_I, and WS_{MI} as policy instruments.

The initial specification of the equations is given below. In actual model construction, these would be subject to some modification, based on the results of initial statistical estimation.

The equations of the structural system are:

$$E_a = \gamma_{10} + \beta_{12}\, Em + \gamma_{11}\, W_{na} + \gamma_{12}\, R + \gamma_{14}\, WT + \gamma_{15}\, WS_I + e_1 \quad (9\text{-}58)$$

$$E_m = \gamma_{20} + \beta_{23}\, E_r + \beta_{25}\, P + \gamma_{24}\, WT + \gamma_{26}\, WS_{MI} + e_2 \quad (9\text{-}59)$$

$$E_r = \gamma_{30} + \beta_{32}\, Em + \beta_{35}\, P + \gamma_{33}\, D + e_3 \quad (9\text{-}60)$$

$$E \equiv Ea + Em + Er \quad (9\text{-}61)$$

$$P = \gamma_{50} + \beta_{51}\, Ea + \beta_{52}\, Em + \beta_{53}\, Er + \gamma_{57}\, WR + e_5 \quad (9\text{-}62)$$

where e_i represent random errors or disturbance terms. (The subscripts on the coefficients (i, j) indicate equation i and variable j of a class. That is, β_{12} would be the coefficient on the second of the five jointly dependent variables for the first equation; γ_{54} would be the coefficient in the fifth equation on the fourth of the predetermined variables.)

Equations (9-58) - (9-60) explain employment change in the agricultural, manufacturing, and residentiary sectors; (9-61) is an identity stating that total change in regional employment equals the sum of employment change in the three sectors listed above; and equation (9-62) explains population change as a function of employment change and the existence of water based recreation. Following Muth's general equilibrium model,[23] employment and population are simultaneously determined, rather than employment being determined independently of population and then having the latter defined as unidirectional function of the former, as is characteristic of export-base type models. With the exception of the introduction of water resource variables in Equations (9-58), (9-60), and (9-62), the model is fairly standard. Therefore discussion of specific equations will be confined to the role played by the water variables, and the various theories or hypotheses that might be tested by these equations.

Both the water transport dummy and the irrigation water index enter the agricultural employment equation. The coefficient of the latter (γ_{15}) is hypothesized to be positive in that the availability of irrigation water will allow production (and, therefore, employment) in areas where climatic conditions, primarily lack of rainfall, would otherwise not allow it. Average annual rainfall (R) is included as a predetermined variable, so that the relationship between irrigation supply and employment can be estimated holding rainfall constant. This is important, as rainfall is an important determinant of the level of agricultural activity. The sign of the coefficient on WT could be either positive or negative, depending on the relative labor intensity of water-transportable crops.

It should prove useful to examine the structure of this econometric model using the matrix algebra approach described earlier. Consider the following vectors and matrices:

$$
B = \begin{bmatrix}
1 & -\beta_{12} & 0 & 0 & 0 \\
0 & 1 & -\beta_{23} & 0 & -\beta_{25} \\
0 & -\beta_{32} & 1 & 0 & -\beta_{35} \\
-1 & -1 & -1 & 1 & 0 \\
-\beta_{51} & -\beta_{52} & -\beta_{53} & 0 & 1
\end{bmatrix}, \quad
y = \begin{bmatrix}
E_a \\
E_m \\
E_r \\
E \\
P
\end{bmatrix}
\tag{9-63}
$$

$$
\Gamma = \begin{bmatrix}
\gamma_{10} & \gamma_{11} & \gamma_{12} & 0 & \gamma_{14} & \gamma_{15} & 0 & 0 \\
\gamma_{20} & 0 & 0 & 0 & \gamma_{24} & 0 & \gamma_{26} & 0 \\
\gamma_{30} & 0 & 0 & \gamma_{33} & 0 & 0 & 0 & 0 \\
0 & 0 & 0 & 0 & 0 & 0 & 0 & 0 \\
\gamma_{50} & 0 & 0 & 0 & 0 & 0 & 0 & \gamma_{57}
\end{bmatrix}, \quad
x = \begin{bmatrix}
1 \\
W \\
R \\
D \\
WT \\
WS_I \\
WS_{MI} \\
WR
\end{bmatrix},
$$

$$
e = \begin{bmatrix}
e_1 \\
e_2 \\
e_3 \\
0 \\
e_4
\end{bmatrix}
\tag{9-64}
$$

Now the system described by Equations (9–58) - (9–62) can be written as

$$B\,y = \Gamma\,X + e \qquad\qquad (9\text{–}65)$$

and the reduced form is formed by

$$y = B^{-1}\,\Gamma\,X + B^{-1}\,e \qquad\qquad (9\text{–}66)$$

As discussed below, the reduced form equations are particularly useful in a policy application of the model. To analyze specific parts of the model and its general structure, reference will be made to the original structural equations. Assume that wheat, corn, and soybeans are amenable to water transportation. As these tend to be relatively labor-extensive crops, we might expect the coefficient (γ_{14}) to be negative. Given the possible ambiguity in interpreting the coefficient of WT, it might be useful to include an equation for net farm income in the region. In such a function, a significant positive coefficient on WT would tend to confirm the hypothesis that the availability of water transportation in the region has a positive effect on farm income, because it provides a low-cost transport alternative and broadens the range of choice in terms of cropping patterns.

Two water variables, water transport (WT) and the index for municipal and industrial supply (WS_{MI}), are included in the manufacturing employment Equation (9–59). If the availability of good quality, low cost water is, in fact, a significant locational factor for industry, the coefficient on the supply variable would be expected to be positive and statistically significant. This test would probably be stronger if two equations were estimated, one for water-oriented manufacturing industries and a second for all other manufacturing. Similarly, the coefficient on WT is expected to be positive. The availability of water transportation should have a positive influence on the growth of manufacturing employment, both in industries which can use water transport for shipping output or for bringing in raw materials, and in other industries which, although not oriented to water transport, are linked to those that are.

The inclusion of the water recreation index (WR) in the population Equation (9–62) is designed to test the hypothesis that people are attracted to an area because of its inventory of recreational assets, especially those that are water-related.

In addition to providing a test of several hypotheses concerning the relationship between water resources and regional economic growth, the estimated model can be used in a policy context to predict the growth impacts of improving the quality or increasing the stock of certain water resources. An analysis of reduced form equations can identify the probable total impact, both direct and indirect, of a given change in any predetermined variable on the particular jointly dependent variable under study.

A time-series model estimated for a specific, rather than typical region is well suited for forecasting economic activity under alternative assumptions concerning changes in predetermined variables. The effect of improvement in water quality or increase in supply would be entered into the model by increasing the index (WS_{MI}) at some future time period. Levels of activity following such a change could be compared to a neutral or base-line forecast to estimate the net impact of that water investment in the region under study.

Simulation Models

Simulation techniques have been used to recreate, describe, and/or predict the behavior of physical or socioeconomic systems.[24] Essentially,

> . . . simulation of a system or an organism is the operation of a model or simulator which is a representation of the system or organism. The model is amenable to manipulation which would be impossible, too expensive, or unpractical to perform as the entity it portrays. The operation of the model can be studied, and, from it, properties concerning the behavior of the actual system or its subsystem can be inferred.[25]

The feasibility and popularity of this technique are enhanced by the rapid introduction of new computer technology and the limited capacity and flexibility of normative programming techniques. Indeed simulation may provide a useful realistic alternative and/or complement to other techniques. Simply stated, the essence of simulation is to reproduce the behavior of a system in every important respect.

Adequate definition of simulation technique is rendered difficult because of an inclination to associate the technique with its typical applications. Further, separately identified analytic techniques, such as single and multiple equation econometric systems and optimization models are merely specialized or somewhat restricted forms of simulation. For these reasons, subsequent discussion in this chapter is restricted to a specific application of the technique which seems especially pertinent to a consideration of the impacts of water development on subnational economies.

The Susquehanna study [26] was designed to examine the demands that the economy of the Susquehanna Basin will place on the river during the next 50 years. Simulation was judged to be the technique best suited for this purpose because a very large number of variables were required in making long-run economic and water use projections; long run interactions among resources and demographic and economic variables made it essential to include their feedback and time-related relationships; and river basin planning is too complex a problem to be treated realistically by more conventional optimizing techniques, primarily because of the necessity of permitting consideration of a mixture of goals and objectives.

After the model was developed, it was used to make 50-year simulations for each of the nine subregions.[k] Dimensions or output variables arrayed over this time span included population, migration rates, employment, and per capita income levels. Three additional sets of experiments were conducted with the model. The first was designed to weigh the impact of three alternative levels of river development including the present systems of works, an elaborate level consisting of all known dams and reservoirs recommended by any reputable group, and a moderate level consisting of a selection of works from the elaborate system.

The second experiment involved changing several elements in the model one at a time and tracing their impacts on output variables through the 50-year simulation. This provided some test of the sensitivity of many of the values and relationships which were estimated statistically or judgmentally. Relationships tested in this manner included migration rates, birth rate-unemployment relationship, regional labor force-export relationship, market access, and labor participation-unemployment relationship.

A final set of experiments involving alteration of combinations of the individual experiments gave rise to unusual projections of the output variables in some regions. From the results of these experiments, it was concluded in the Susquehanna study that considerable danger is inherent in assuming that similar public investments and policies will affect different areas in a similar manner. The results of this experiment also tend to support the contention of this book, that the impacts of water development must be viewed within a regional context which makes possible identification of differences in their characteristics and in differential income, employment, and population impacts.

The authors concluded that simulation models of the type constructed for analysis of the Susquehanna Basin offer great promise in terms of advancing the state of the art in regional economics and river basin analysis. In particular, they integrate the treatment of population, employment, and resource variables; thus tending to move planning away from a simple requirements approach.

Notes

1. Hollis B. Chenery and Paul G. Clark, *Interindustry Economics* (New York: John Wiley and Sons, 1959).
2. Wassily Leontief, *The Structure of the American Economy, 1919-1939* (New York: Oxford University Press, 1951).

[k]Subregions were delineated using a "trading-area and labor market areas" concept, thus identifying relatively independent spatial entities (economic activity). The authors assert that this was desirable because river works are planned for specific locations within the basin, and because the characteristics of economic activity varied significantly from one area to another. The similarity of their approach and the recommendation of this book concerning the use of FEA's or FEA-type regions appears obvious.

3. Walter Isard, "Interregional and Regional Input-Output Analysis: A Model of a Space Economy," *The Review of Economics and Statistics*, XXXIII, 4 (November, 1951) 318–328.

4. For examples of such studies see: H.C. Davis, *Economic Evaluation of Water, Part V: Multiregional Input-Output Techniques and Western Water Resources Development*, Water Resources Center contribution No. 125 (Berkeley: Sanitary Engineering Research Laboratory, University of California, February, 1968).

   Jona Bargur, *Economic Evaluation of Water, Part VI: A Dynamic Inter-Regional Input-Output Programming Model of the California and Western States Water Economy*, WRC contribution No. 128 (Berkeley: SERL, University of California, June, 1969).

   E.M. Lofting and P.H. McGauhey, *Economic Evaluation of Water, Part III: An Interindustry Analysis of the California Water Economy*, WRC contribution No. 67 (Berkeley: SERL, University of California, January, 1963).

5. Estimates of water withdrawal coefficients by industry are provided in: Kenneth MacKichan and J.C. Kammerer, *Estimated Water Use in the United States, 1960*, U.S. Geological Survey Circular No. 456 (Washington, D.C.: U.S. Department of the Interior, 1961).

   Bureau of the Census, *Water Use in Manufacturing*, 1963 (Washington, D.C.: U.S. Department of Commerce, 1965).

6. Davis, *Economic Evaluation of Water, Part V*.

7. Robert L. Allen and Donald A. Watson, *The Structure of the Oregon Economy* (Eugene: The University of Oregon Press, 1965).

8. Bernard Udis, ed., *An Interindustry Analysis of the Colorado River Basin in 1960 with Projections to 1980 and 2010*, nine volumes (Boulder: Federal Water Pollution Control Administration and University of Colorado, June 1968).

9. Basic references on programming include: George Hadley, *Linear Programming* (Reading, Massachusetts: Addison-Wesley, 1962).

   Abraham W. Charnes, W.W. Cooper, and H. Henderson, *An Introduction to Linear Programming* (New York: John Wiley and Sons, 1953).

   For a specific application of linear programming to economics, see: Robert A. Dorfman, Paul A. Samuelson, and Robert M. Solow, *Linear Programming and Economic Analysis* (New York: McGraw-Hill, 1958).

10. Charles L. Leven and R.B. Read, *A River, A Region, and a Research Problem* (Alexandria, Va.: U.S. Army Engineer Institute for Water Resources, March 1971).

11. *Ibid.*, p. 159.

12. Lofting and McGauhey, *Economic Evaluation of Water, Part III*.

13. *Ibid.*, pp. 72–73.

14. Saul H. Hymans and Harold Shapiro, "The DHL-III Quarterly Econometric Model of the U.S. Economy," *The Outlook for 1970*, 17th Annual Conference On the Economic Outlook, Ann Arbor, University of Michigan, November 20–21, 1969.

15. Maurice Liebenberg, Albert Hirsch, and Joel Popkin, "A Quarterly Econo-

metric Model of the United States: A Progress Report," *Survey of Current Business* XLVI, 5 (May, 1966) 13–39.

16. F.G. Adams and M.K. Evans, *Economic Forecasting with the Wharton-EFU Model: The Five Year Forecasting Record*, discussion paper No. 78 (Philadelphia: Department of Economics, University of Pennsylvania, 1968). M.K. Evans and L.R. Klein, *The Wharton Econometric Forecasting Model* (2nd ed., Philadelphia: University of Pennsylvania, 1968).

17. Frederick W. Bell, "An Econometric Forecasting Model for a Region," *Journal of Regional Science*, VII, 2 (Winter, 1967) 105–127.

18. R. Burton and J. Dyckman, *A Quarterly Economic Forecasting Model for the State of California*, (Berkeley: Center for Planning Development, Research Institute of Urban and Regional Development, University of California, 1967).

19. For a comprehensive review of these statistical estimation methods, see: Johnston, *Econometric Methods.*
Arthur S. Goldberger, *Econometric Theory* (New York: John Wiley and Sons, 1964).

20. For an example of the use of programming techniques for parameter estimation, see: D.F. Aigner and S.F. Chu,""On Estimating the Industry Production Function," *American Economic Review*, LVIII, 4 (September, 1968) 826–839.

21. Henri Theil, *Applied Economic Forecasting* (Chicago: Rand McNally, 1966).

22. Jan Tinbergen, *On the Theory of Economic Policy* (Amsterdam: North Holland Publishing, 1966).

23. Richard F. Muth, *Differential Growth Among Large U.S. Cities*, Institute for Urban and Regional Studies, working paper No. 15 (St. Louis: Washington University, 1968).

24. The following symposium papers summarize standard application of simulation techniques: G.H. Orcutt, "Simulation of Economic Systems," *The American Economic Review*, L, 5 (December 1960) 893–907.
G.P.E. Clarkson and Herbert A. Simon, "Simulation of Group Behavior," *The American Economic Review*, L, 5 (December, 1960) 920–932.
Martin Shubik, "Simulation of Industry and Firm," *The American Economic Review*, L, 5 (December 1960) 908–919.
A discussion of recent developments and applications is provided by:
J.W. Forrester, *Industrial Dynamics* (Cambridge, Mass.: The MIT Press, 1961).
J.W. Forrester, *Urban Dynamics* (Cambridge, Mass.: The MIT Press, 1969). and Arthur Maas, M. Hufschmidt, R. Dorfman, H.A. Thomas, Jr., S.A. Marglin, and G.M. Fair. *Design of Water Resource Systems* (Cambridge, Mass.: Harvard University Press, 1962).

25. Martin Shubik, "Simulation of the Industry and the Firm," *American Economic Review*, L, 5 (December, 1960), 908–918.

26. H.R. Hamilton, S.E. Goldstone, J.W. Milliman, A.L. Pugh, III, E.B. Roberts, and A. Zellner, *Systems Simulation for Regional Analysis: An Application to River Basin Planning* (Cambridge, Mass.: The MIT Press, 1969).

10 Illustrations of Impact Analysis

To illustrate and apply the concepts already developed, a set of four hypothetical case studies of the economic impacts of water investments will be developed. These cases will illustrate a variety of resource situations, investment types, and analytical techniques.

Water investments will be classified by the type of service generated (i.e., power, recreation, etc.), and, for the illustrations, only single-purpose projects will be considered. Three types of regions will be considered: an urban-industrial complex; a rural-agricultural area; and a region in the midst of changing from a predominantly agricultural area to one where manufacturing employment is dominant. The following combinations of investments and regions will be analyzed:

1. Increased municipal and industrial water supply in an urban-industrial area
2. A recreation project in a rural-agricultural area
3. Development of a navigable waterway serving a transitional region
4. An irrigation project in an agricultural region.

The following assumptions will be made: perfect competition in factor and product markets; initial equilibrium in the multiregion economy; constant prices, other than those for the service provided by the water project; given technical conditions of production, the same in all regions for a given industry; and the same price elasticity of demand for any commodity in all regions.

Case 1. Increasing Supply in an Urban-Industrial Region

It will be assumed that except for water supply this region has the potential for above average growth in population and employment. It is a water-short area, defined as one where, given the technical conditions of production, the price schedule for water, and the capacity of the city's system to provide water, further water consumption by manufacturing firms and public utilities is constrained by inadequate water supply. It will be useful to consider the impact on output, employment, factor prices, and total factor returns, both with and without the project, which is assumed to double the available water supply.

These effects can be estimated directly from the production function, while the impacts on welfare measures, structure, and environment will be inferred. Again, it should be emphasized that this section is concerned only with the direct effects confined to the water-oriented manufacturing industries.

Consider the following production function:

$$Y = A(t) K_1^{\alpha} K_2^{\delta} N^{\beta} \tag{10-1}$$

where Y represents output; K_1, nonwater capital inputs; K_2, water; and N, labor. The marginal products of the factors are given by

$$\partial Y / \partial K_1 = \frac{\alpha A(t) K_2^{\delta} N^{\beta}}{K_1^{1-\alpha}} = MP_{K_1} \tag{10-2}$$

$$\partial Y / \partial K_2 = \frac{\delta A(t) K_1^{\alpha} N^{\beta}}{K_2^{1-\delta}} = MP_{K_2} \tag{10-3}$$

$$\partial Y / \partial N = \frac{\beta A(t) K_1^{\alpha} K_2^{\delta}}{N^{1-\beta}} = MP_N \tag{10-4}$$

and, given the above assumptions, these marginal products also represent the real prices of these factors. Assume that the production function exhibits constant returns to scale and that each production elasticity is positive, (i.e., $\alpha + \beta + \delta = 1$ and $\alpha, \beta, \delta > 0$).

In this region increased output will be forthcoming only by increasing the levels of nonwater capital (K_1) and labor. This will tend to lead to changes in marginal product functions and to higher average cost functions relative to regions where all three factors are variable. Assume that N and K_1 are increased proportionately. Clearly the marginal product of water will increase. As long as $\beta + \alpha < 1$, as implied by the assumptions of constant returns to scale and $\delta > 0$, proportionate increases in both nonwater capital and labor will cause downward shifts in the marginal product functions of those factors. As $\beta < 1 - \alpha$, implying $\alpha < 1 - \beta$, the denominator of both functions (10-2) and (10-4) will increase more than the numerator.

That the cost function is at least as high with the water input fixed as with ample supplies of water is obvious. The profit-maximizing producer's range of choice of input combinations is at least as great and typically greater in the latter case. This situation can be analyzed by comparing cost functions under alternative assumptions about water supply. Assume that markets are perfectly competitive, and that prices are constant initially. Assume from Equation

(10-1) that conventional marginal products can be derived, and that they are declining in the relevant stages. Total cost will be minimized by using those levels of factors where

$$MC_Y = \frac{P_{K_1}}{MP_{K_1}} = \frac{P_{K_2}}{MP_{K_2}} = \frac{P_N}{MP_N} \qquad (10\text{-}5)$$

and the firm will be in equilibrium, or, said alternatively,

$$MC_Y^{K_1} = MC_Y^{K_2} = MC_Y^{N} \qquad (10\text{-}6)$$

Now suppose an autonomous rise in P_N, then

$$\frac{P_{K_1}}{MP_{K_1}} < \frac{P_N}{MP_N} \text{ or } MC_Y^{K_1} < MC_Y^{N} \qquad (10\text{-}7)$$

and

$$\frac{P_{K_2}}{MP_{K_2}} < \frac{P_N}{MP_N} \text{ or } MC_Y^{K_2} < MC_Y^{N} \qquad (10\text{-}8)$$

The firm is no longer minimizing cost. To restore equilibrium MP_{K_1} and MP_{K_2} must be reduced relative to MP_N. But suppose that K_2 (water) cannot be increased so as to reduce MP_{K_2}. Then the firm cannot increase output by the least costly method and the cost curves must be higher than would be the case if water (K_2) application could be increased.

The result of a rising cost function will be a reduction in the supply area served by this industry, implying decreased output and employment, assuming that other regions are not faced with water supply or other constraints and, therefore, operate under a stable set of cost conditions. The supply area for region i is composed of all those markets for which

$$P_i + T_i < P_j + T_j \qquad \begin{matrix} j = 1 \\ j \neq i \end{matrix}, \ldots, n \qquad (10\text{-}9)$$

that is, where the delivered cost, the sum of the price at the production source (P_i) and the transport cost to the market in question (T_i), is less than from any other source. As the average cost function shifts upward, the competitive conditions (price equal to marginal cost) imply that price (P_i) will be rising, thus causing some markets to shift their source of supply to a different region. The initial decline in output and employment will lead to multiple declines (indirect impacts) in output and employment in many, if not all, other industries in the region.

From a national perspective, part of the output decline in the water-short area will be offset by output increases in other regions—most likely those which are both close to the study area and in a position to capture the markets at the periphery of the original supply areas. The price elasticity of demand, assumed constant among regions, will play an important role here. If the demand functions are perfectly inelastic, the decline in output should be offset completely by increases in other regions. If the functions are not completely inelastic, only part of the decline will be offset because delivered price must have increased in at least one market. The size of the reduction in output at the national level will be a function of the magnitude of price increase and the elasticity. In the Leven study[1] the regional changes in activity were exactly offsetting. The cost reduction in that study, which was concerned with increased availability and decreased cost of water, was insufficient to cause an increase in the quantity of output demanded. In that analysis, the only other region affected was that one which sold its output in the region closest to the project area.

For those industries where water is a significant input, an investment which creates additional water supply at the same price as before should enable the region to maintain its share of the market. If these water supplies are offered at lower prices, there should be a decline in production costs, possibly leading to price reductions and, thus, to an expanded market share and increased output and employment. Also, there should be relative substitution of water for labor and nonwater capital, increasing the marginal production function of those factors.[a] If factor supply curves are assumed constant, factor prices and total factor returns should increase. Initially, the cost advantage which allows an increase in market share should also lead to the existence of economic profit in the affected sector. This, in turn, should stimulate the location of new firms in the region, attracted by the profit possibilities. Increased competition from those firms should tend to eliminate the excess profit over a period of time.

Thus, the water supply project will either arrest possible declines in output and employment by allowing the regional industry to maintain its market share (this is the case where the price of water is not changed), or facilitate increased output and employment by providing a necessary input (water) at a reduced cost. In either event, per capita income in the region should be above the level that would have prevailed if the project had not been built. Furthermore, there probably would have been increased unemployment without the project (this would depend on employment conditions in other industries—

---

[a]This should be clear from examination of Equations (10-2) and (10-4). Increases in K_2, holding K_1 and N constant, will shift these functions upward.

could they have absorbed the labor released from the water-constrained industry?), and an unfavorable change in the distribution of income as increased unemployment shifted families out of middle income classes ($5,000 to $10,000 per year) into lower income classes.

The environmental impacts are not clear. If the industry under study is a major polluter of air and/or water, failure to make the water supply investment might lead to reduction in pollution levels, particularly when the multiple indirect impacts are included. Conversely, the increased economic activity associated with making the investment, particularly if water costs are reduced, may lead to increases in the level of pollution. However, this possibility is largely irrelevant. Investments of the type described here, which are designed to facilitate increased output and employment, should probably not be considered part of the pollution problem nor part of an antipollution program. Increased pollution levels indirectly associated with water supply creating investments should be viewed and dealt with as social costs not borne by the polluting firm. Programs designed to control such pollution should probably be disassociated with investments intended to increase factor supplies and/or quality.

Case 2. Recreation Project–
Agricultural Region

Here consideration is given to the impact of developing a recreation-oriented water resource (presumably a lake, reservoir, or river) in a primarily agricultural area. Assume that the single purpose of this investment is to provide recreational services for area residents and tourists, although this is likely to be a special case. Alternatively, assume that only one purpose of a multiple-purpose project is being considered, although the possibility of development interactions among the various services generated by the resource may alter the impacts.

The region under study is predominantly agricultural. Nonagricultural activities are confined to the so-called nonbasic sectors (i.e., retail, wholesale, services, local government, etc.) and perhaps some employment in agricultural processing industries, such as meat packing and canning. Assume also that prior to the time this investment was made there had been no water-based recreation site of any significance in the region. The input-output table for the project area, shown in Table 10-1, describes the regional economy.[b] Agri-

---

[b]This table is set up in a slightly heterodox manner. The technical coefficients (a_{ij}), the input from industry i per dollar of output of industry j, are shown in the upper left-hand part of the table rather than interindustry transactions. This will facilitate comparison of the I-O structure before and after the investment, in that the technical coefficients should remain relatively constant, whereas most interindustry transactions will tend to change when any final demand is changed. Also, the entries in the next to the last row are value added coefficients (value added per unit of output) rather than total value added.

Table 10-1
Regional Input-Output Table Before Water Investment

Industry Producing	1 Agriculture	2 Manufacturing-Agriculture Processing	3 Other Manufacturing	4 Recreation	5 Miscellaneous	Domestic Final Demand	Exports
1. Agriculture	a_{11}	a_{12}	0	0	a_{15}	F_1	E_1
2. Manufacturing-agriculture processing	a_{21}	a_{22}	0	0	a_{25}	F_2	E_2
3. Other manufacturing	0	0	0	0	0	0	0
4. Recreation	0	0	0	0	0	0	0
5. Miscellaneous	a_{51}	a_{52}	0	0	a_{55}	F_5	0
Value added	v_1	v_2	0	0	v_5		
Imports	M_1	M_2	M_3	M_4	0		

culture is the major employing and exporting industry; agricultural processing is the only other industry exporting anything from the region. Before the project there is no regional output from the water-recreation industry. There are imports of recreational services from other regions as some residents of the project area travel to other areas to consume these services. Other imports include those from the manufacturing sectors, both agricultural processors and others.

The magnitude of the developmental impacts will depend on a number of factors. What proportion of project area residents will consume recreational services at the new reservoir? Will this recreation resource be of sufficient size and quality to attract recreationists from other regions? How long can the average visitor be expected to stay? What are his spending habits? Will there be sufficient recreation activity (as measured by visitor-days by both project area residents and tourists) to allow the development of a recreation industry in the project area? If such an industry does develop, will ownership and employment accrue largely to area residents or will there be a sizeable in-migration of capital and labor?

Each of these questions raises a number of possibilities for the development of the region, and each should be discussed in more detail. Upon completion of the project, those residents who use the resource for recreation probably will be enjoying higher levels of utility than they were previously. All residents, of course, will have an expanded choice set in the sense that the resource is there if they should want to use it. This will be true of nonproject area recreationists as well; they, too, have an expanded range of choice with regard to the stock of consumer resources, although their use of that resource may be constrained by the travel required.

The source of funds spent for recreation has important implications for national efficiency considerations. If recreation investment in the project area simply represents money that would have been spent to develop recreational services in other regions, the net multiplier effect on national income will be approximately zero, as expansion of activity in the project area will simply represent activity displaced from other areas. If this spending represents diversion of funds from nonrecreational expenditures, the impact on national income is not clear. It would depend on the relative multipliers associated with such spending. At the other extreme, if all new spending for recreation comes out of the saving stream, there would be a sizeable multiplier effect on national income.[c]

Within the project area there will very likely be some displacement of activity. Some income which had been spent at the local theatre or bowling

---

[c]In the associated studies by Leven [2] and Tolley,[3] the two ends of this range were analyzed. That is, the recreation impact of water investment was analyzed under the alternative assumptions that all funds spent in the project area came out of saving, or that all funds would have been spent in other regions for recreational services.

alley may now be spent on boats, motors, gasoline, etc.—goods that probably are produced outside the region. Spending on such durable goods suggests that there will be substantial changes in the pattern of imports (e.g., a substitution of boats, motors, and trailers for automobiles). These impacts on other regions are beyond the scope of this discussion, but could be analyzed in detail using an interregional input-output model of the type described in Chapter 9.

The ability of the water resource to attract recreationists from other regions, particularly those who will stay several days or perhaps even several weeks, will be critical in the development of a recreation-tourist industry in the project area. This industry, defined broadly to include motels, restaurants, and suppliers of recreation equipment (e.g., boats, motors, camping gear, etc.), is likely to develop only if large numbers of people come into the project area to spend at least several days. Clearly, there will be little additional motel or restaurant volume generated by increased recreational activity of project area residents.

Assuming such an industry does develop, the effect on the structure of the local economy might best be estimated by analyzing changes in the region's input-output table. For example, the recreation-tourist industry, previously nonexistent in the project area, develops and becomes the third export sector in the region. This industry is presumed to be directly linked to the "miscellaneous" sector, which, in turn, is linked to the agriculture and agricultural processing sectors, so that increased final demand for output of the recreation industry should lead to positive indirect impacts on all of the region's industries.

The new structure is depicted in an adjusted input-output table (Table 10-2). There is now regional output from the recreation sector, as indicated by final demand from within the region, (F_4^1), and exports, (E_4^1).[d] Imports of recreational services, (M_4^1), are lower now as residents need not leave the area to consume such services. There are interindustry transactions between the recreation and miscellaneous sectors, $(a_{45}^1$ and $a_{54}^1)$ as well as transactions within the recreation industry, (a_{44}^1). Of course, there is now value added originating in the recreation sector, (V_4^1).[e]

If the project is of sufficient scale, the first round of development impacts, together with a set of construction impacts, may lead to employment and population increases sufficient to allow the development of some small-scale manufacturing activity (sector 3 in the input-output framework). Such industries might produce output for other regional industries, particularly the recreation industry, as well as consumer goods. It is likely that development of this industry would be limited to those operations with low threshold levels, or equivalently, where most economies of scale are captured by a relatively small plant. Some output from these sectors would probably be exported to neighboring regions.

---

[d]The superscript is used to denote elements of the I-O structure that have changed during the first round of impacts associated with the project.

[e]There might also be changes in other final demands and imports as residents' preferences change, but, for the sake of clarity, these will be assumed as constant.

Table 10-2
Regional Input-Output Table After Initial Effects of the Water Investment

Industry Producing \ Industry Purchasing	1 Agriculture	2 Manufacturing-Agriculture Processing	3 Other Manufacturing	4 Recreation	5 Miscellaneous	Domestic Final Demand	Exports
1. Agriculture	a_{11}	a_{12}	0	0	a_{15}	F_1	E_1
2. Manufacturing-agriculture processing	a_{21}	a_{22}	0	a_{24}^1	a_{25}	F_2	E_2
3. Other manufacturing	0	0	0	0	0	0	0
4. Recreation	0	0	0	a_{44}^1	a_{45}^1	F_4^1	E_4^1
5. Miscellaneous	a_{51}	a_{52}	0	a_{54}^1	a_{55}	F_5	0
Value added	v_1	v_2	0	v_4^1	v_5		
Imports	M_1	M_2	M_3	M_4^1	0		

The changes in the region's I-O structure associated with this second development stage include the addition of regional final demand (F_3^2) and exports (E_3^2) associated with the manufacturing sector, interindustry transactions between this industry and all other industry as indicated by the technical coefficients $(a_{31}^2, \ldots, a_{35}^2)$, and a change in imports of manufactured goods (M_3^2). This change in imports could be positive or negative as imports of those goods produced locally would probably decrease, but because of increased regional income, imports of other manufactured goods might increase. These changes in structure are outlined in Table 10-3.

Output from each of the region's industries at each stage of the development process can be determined by solving the input-output system for the vector of industry outputs (X). This vector (X^0), together with the matrix of technical coefficients (A^0) and the vector of final demand (F^0), depicting the region's economy before the water investment, are shown below:

$$X^0 = \begin{bmatrix} X_1 \\ X_2 \\ X_5 \end{bmatrix}, \qquad A^0 = \begin{bmatrix} A_{11} & A_{12} & A_{15} \\ A_{21} & A_{22} & A_{25} \\ A_{51} & A_{52} & A_{55} \end{bmatrix}, \qquad F^0 = \begin{bmatrix} F_1 + E_1 \\ F_2 + E_2 \\ F_5 \end{bmatrix} \quad (10\text{-}10)$$

Output of the region's industries is determined by

$$X^0 = (I_3 - A^0)^{-1} F^0 \qquad (10\text{-}11)$$

where I_3 is a (3×3) identity matrix. Total value added, (VA), in the region would be determined by

$$VA = V'X^0 \qquad (10\text{-}12)$$

where V is (3×1) column vector of coefficients indicating value added per unit of output in each of the region's industries.

Assuming the project is of sufficient size and quality, the region's economic structure will expand as the recreation industry develops.

$$X^1 = \begin{bmatrix} X_1 \\ X_2 \\ X_4 \\ X_5 \end{bmatrix}, \qquad A^1 = \begin{bmatrix} a_{11} & a_{12} & 0 & a_{15} \\ a_{21} & a_{22} & a_{24}^1 & a_{25} \\ 0 & 0 & a_{44}^1 & a_{45} \\ a_{51} & a_{52} & a_{54}^1 & a_{55} \end{bmatrix}, \qquad F^1 = \begin{bmatrix} F_1 + E_1 \\ F_2 + E_2 \\ F_4^1 + E_4^1 \\ F_5 \end{bmatrix} \quad (10\text{-}13)$$

Table 10-3
Regional Input-Output Structure After Second Round of Development Impacts

Industry Producing \ Industry Purchasing	1 Agriculture	2 Manufacturing-Agriculture Processing	3 Other Manufacturing	4 Recreation	5 Miscellaneous	Domestic Final Demand	Exports
1. Agriculture	a_{11}	a_{12}	a_{12}	0	a_{15}	F_1	E_1
2. Manufacturing-agriculture processing	a_{21}	a_{22}	a_{23}^2	a_{25}	a	F_2	E_2
3. Other manufacturing	a_{31}^2	a_{32}^2	a_{33}^2	a_{34}^2	a_{35}^2	F_3^2	E_3^2
4. Recreation	0	0	0	a_{44}^1	a_{45}^1	F_4^1	E_4^1
5. Miscellaneous	a_{51}	a_{52}	a_{53}	a_{54}	a_{55}	F_5	0
Value added	v_1	v_2	v_3^2	v_4^1	v_5		
Imports	M_1	M_2	M_3^1	M_4^1	0		

and, again, regional output by industry is given by

$$X^1 = (I_4 - A^1)^{-1} F^1 \tag{10-14}$$

Value added is estimated as above except that the value added vector is now dimensioned (4×1) to accommodate the new industry.

Finally, if there is a second round of developmental impacts, the structure appears as

$$X^2 = \begin{bmatrix} X_1 \\ X_2 \\ X_3 \\ X_4 \\ X_5 \end{bmatrix}, \qquad A^2 = \begin{bmatrix} a_{11} & a_{12} & a_{13}^2 & 0 & a_{15} \\ a_{21} & a_{22} & a_{23}^2 & a_{24}^1 & a_{25} \\ a_{31}^2 & a_{32}^2 & a_{33}^2 & a_{34}^2 & a_{35}^2 \\ 0 & 0 & 0 & a_{44}^1 & a_{45}^1 \\ a_{51} & a_{52} & a_{53}^2 & a_{54}^1 & a_{55} \end{bmatrix} \qquad F^2 = \begin{bmatrix} F_1 + E_1 \\ F_2 + E_2 \\ F_3^2 + E_3^2 \\ F_4^1 + E_4^1 \\ F_5 \end{bmatrix} \tag{10-15}$$

with output being determined by

$$X^2 = (I_5 - A^2)^{-1} F^2 \tag{10-16}$$

Several important questions should be raised in evaluating the change in welfare of project area residents. Will there be significant intersectoral shifts of labor and capital within the region? In particular, will there be an acceleration of movement of labor from agriculture to other employment in manufacturing or recreation? The magnitude of such shifts will depend largely on the relative returns of the various sectors. In an agricultural area characterized by above average farm income, it is questionable that there would be significant movement of labor to employment in the recreation industry, which is not, in general, a high wage industry. In a low income region, one which undoubtedly had been experiencing migration from the farm and region, the provision of alternative employment, especially if some manufacturing activity begins, will probably accelerate these intersectoral shifts.

Clearly, the economic characteristics and structure of the region are important. In a high-income region, there is little opportunity for income gains by reallocating labor among industries. Therefore, it would be expected that the direct and indirect effects of the water project, leading to an increase in total regional activity, would be associated with relatively large immigration of labor. In the low income agricultural region, a larger part of the investment-induced employment increase would accrue to area residents who have left low income employment, primarily in agriculture.

It should be clear, however, that Stage II impacts are probably only achieved by very large projects, especially those coordinated with the development of other types of recreational resources, e.g., state and national parks; private tourist attractions; and, possibly, highways. The latter, obviously, facilitate the consumption of recreational services. For the typical reservoir or lake, which has nothing else to recommend it and is not located on a major tourist route, it is unlikely that the region will feel more than Stage I impacts, and these will probably result in only small changes in regional economic structure, with little change in output or employment.

Case 3. Waterborne Transportation in an Industrializing Region

Transportation systems and relative rates among transport alternatives have had a significant effect on the growth and spatial structure of the United States economy. In the early decades of the industrial revolution, the location of the primary transport modes, the railroad and, to a lesser extent, canals, led to a concentration of economic activity in regions serviced by these transportation systems. The fact that until recently the larger share of the country's industrial production was concentrated in the northeastern quadrant of the country probably could have been predicted by examining railroad routes. The expansion of railroad service to most parts of the U.S., and, even more important, the advent of the motor truck and the development of a comprehensive system of state and national highways, set in motion a decentralization of all forms of economic activity. This is evidenced by the rapid economic growth of the southern, southwestern, and western parts of the country. Not only was there a decentralization of activity among regions, but also within regions, particularly in the larger cities. The speed and flexibility of the motor truck, coupled with the ubiquitous ownership of the automobile, led to rapid development, both residential and industrial, in the outlying or suburban areas of the larger cities. For many producers there was no longer any need to be located in the central core of the city, which, heretofore, had offered the advantage of close proximity to railroad and/or water transportation. Automobile ownership freed individuals from dependence on public transit systems, giving them a greater choice in residential location. Clearly transportation routes, alternative modes of transportation, and rate structures have had a sizeable influence on the spatial distribution of economic activity.

Concern here is with the initial economic effects of constructing a navigable waterway that will link, among other places, an industrializing, formerly agricultural region with one or more of the larger markets of the country or the world. The Arkansas River project, running from eastern Oklahoma across central Arkansas to the Mississippi River, and then, of course, to Memphis and

St. Louis on the north and New Orleans on the south, is a good example of the type of investment and region under study here. Although there will be some recreation and water supply services provided at specific sites along that waterway, its overriding purpose will be provision of transportation services.

Excluding the cities of Tulsa, Fort Smith, and Little Rock, the area to be served is characterized by below average per capita income. Tremendous efforts have been made to raise the income level through changes in the economic structure of the region. The attraction of manufacturing industry and the development of tourist trade account for a large share of the development activity. As indicated by high unemployment rates, the region has a definite labor surplus, and, of those employed, many earn substandard wages in marginal occupations. Thus, the region, which is undergoing rather rapid change in structure, and where there are large potential income gains from intersectoral reallocation of the region's resources, is a most interesting one for the evaluation of such a public investment.

The relative importance of water transportation in the United States is indicated by the data in Table 10–4. Although the volume of commodity shipments made via the more than 25 thousand miles of inland navigation channels has been surpassed by the freight volume shipped by motor trucks or through pipelines, the former still remains a highly significant factor in the movement of goods. Shipments on water more than doubled between 1946 and 1969, and, in the latter year, accounted for almost 16 percent of intercity commodity movements.

An approximation of relative water transport rates is provided by the Barge and Towing Industry Association:[4]

> Barge service costs the shipper an average of three mills per ton mile, with the range being 1-3/4 for some commodities to seven mills for others. Barge services are the biggest transportation bargain in the United States. Only pipelines can offer transportation services at com-

Table 10–4
Intercity Commodity Shipments, Public and Private, 1946 and 1969 (Millions of Ton-Miles)*

	1946	1969
Railroads	602,185	780,000
Inland water**	123,113	300,000
Pipelines	92,490	411,000
Motor truck	66,661	404,000
Air freight	78	3,200

*Taken from the 61st and 84th annual reports of the Interstate Commerce Commission (1947 and 1970), pp. 7 and 77, respectively.
**Includes the Great Lakes.

parable rates. Rail service costs the shipper an average of 15 mills per ton mile. Truck service averages six cents per ton mile. Air freight service is about 20 cents per ton mile.

For many industries, transportation accounts for a significant part of the total cost structure. Transportation costs average over eight percent of the wholesale value of total farm shipments, and about four percent of the wholesale value of manufactured goods. Transportation costs are even higher in the mining and forest products industries than in agriculture. Furthermore, the relative magnitude of transportation costs varies greatly among the industries composing the broad sectors mentioned above. Nichols indicates that nearly 38 percent of the wholesale price of watermelon goes for transportation charges, and similarly, about 15 percent of feed grain wholesale price constitutes transportation charges.[5] Therefore, it is reasonable to expect that investment in navigable waterways could have more influence on regional cost differentials, and, therefore, on industry location, than would projects that increase the supply and/or lower the cost of water.[f]

Products well suited to shipment by water are characterized by low value relative to weight or bulk, no unusual requirements for rapid delivery (e.g., in general, highly perishable foods would clearly not be suitable for water transportation), and susceptibility to highly efficient cargo handling techniques. The first characteristic mentioned suggests that transport costs could account for a large part of the wholesale price of these types of commodities. Leven and Read [6] identified the following industries as being attracted by the availability of water transportation: coal, logging, crude petroleum, sand and gravel, metallic ores, petroleum and coal products, chemicals, and primary metals. They propose that each be included as a separate activity in an input-output study focused on an area having or about to have water transport. In the agricultural sector, grain, grain products, and soybeans are also amenable to water transport.

Leven and Read also point out some of the special problems in assessing the economic effects of changes in transportation costs, routes, and/or capacities:[7]

Analyzing the impact of improved or cheaper water supply or electric power is somewhat different than analyzing the impact of lower transportation costs. The former essentially are equivalent to lowering the production costs of certain activities at particular points in a network of interconnected raw material, production, and market locations. The latter, reducing transportation costs, is equivalent to lowering the costs of moving goods on certain segments of that network. In general, changing transportation costs along particular network segments will

---

[f]Recall the earlier discussion of the relative importance of water costs to industry. In only a few of the water-oriented sectors did water supply costs approach three percent of total costs.

change the whole pattern of raw material supply points for each production location and the pattern of production locations for each
market location; hence, they represent a much more complex kind of
impact than simply lowering the cost of an input at a particular point.

Of the set of services provided by the several types of water resources, it
would appear that transportation could have the greatest development impacts
on a region. In Chapter 6, it was shown that changes in transportation rates
can have a significant effect on factor demand functions, and, hence, on factor
prices and returns. The burden of that argument is on the importance of
transport costs in the price received by the region's producers, and, in turn, on
the factor demand functions. Some producers in the region will find water
transportation suitable for their products, and the effective reduction in transport costs should result in an expanded market area for these outputs. Some
regional firms will experience cost reductions on raw materials from other
regions that can now be shipped more inexpensively via water. This should enable
them to produce at lower cost and sell at lower prices, thereby expanding their
markets. Thus there should be radical changes in the entire distribution system
for final products going out of the region and for raw materials being shipped in.

Other firms should be attracted to the region, both in industries already
represented there and in new industries. The region may have a sizeable potential
in certain of the water-transport oriented industries (e.g., sand, gravel, chemical,
etc.), but not have developed because of a lack of a suitable transport mode.[g]

As in the discussion of the developmental impacts of a recreation project,
an input-output framework can be used to examine the effects associated with
the provision of water transportation services. However, a problem of interpreting the technical coefficients, present in any regional or interregional input-
output model, becomes especially severe when we allow changes in effective
transportation rates.[h] In the simple Leontief model, the technical coefficients,
(a_{ij}), the input from sector i per dollar of output from sector j, are defined by

$$a_{ij} = \frac{Q_{ij}}{\sum\limits_{j} Q_{ij} + P_j} \qquad (10\text{-}17)$$

where Q_{ij} is the total flow between sectors i and j and p_j represents value added

----

[g]It appears, at least from land purchases and statements of management officials, that
such activities are beginning or about to begin along the Arkansas River Project. In addition
to water transport, the region has an abundance of low-cost unskilled labor. Industry seeking
such a combination of water transport and cheap labor should be attracted to this region.

[h]Not only does the regional transportation cost structure change because of the
availability of a navigable channel, it is entirely possible that some rates on other transport
modes, particularly railroads, will be reduced in an effort to remain competitive.

or primary inputs in sector j. In an interregional model, the analogue to Leontief's technical coefficient is

$$a_{ij}^{KL} = \frac{Q_{ij}^{KL}}{\sum\limits_{K}\sum\limits_{i} Q_{ij}^{KL} + p_j^L} \tag{10-18}$$

where Q_{ij}^{KL} is the flow from sector i in region R to sector j in region L, and P_j^L represents primary inputs to sector j of region L. The coefficients a_{ij}^{KL} contain elements of technical production conditions as well as interregional trade characteristics, and, therefore, their interpretation differs significantly from the technical coefficients of the simple Leontief framework. Changes in a_{ij}^{KL} can occur either because of changes in production conditions or through a rearrangement of trading patterns, the latter possibly caused by the availability of a new transport alternative which alters the effective rate structure.

It will be useful to decompose the a_{ij}^{KL} into two coefficients, a pure interregional trade coefficient (s_{ij}^{KL}) and a pure technical coefficient (a_{ij}^L), by

$$(s_{ij}^{KL})\,(a_{ij}^L) = \left(\frac{Q_{ij}^{KL}}{\sum\limits_{K} Q_{ij}^{KL}}\right) \left(\frac{\sum Q_{ij}^{KL}}{\sum\limits_{K}\sum\limits_{i} Q_{ij}^{KL} + p_j^L}\right) \tag{10-19}$$

In an n-industry, p-region economy, the adjusted A matrix will be:

$$\bar{A} = \|s^{KL}\,a^L\| = \begin{bmatrix} s^{11}\,a^1 & s^{12}\,a^2 & \cdots & s^{1p}\,a^p \\ s^{21}\,a^1 & s^{22}\,a^2 & \cdots & s^{2p}\,a^p \\ \cdot & & & \\ \cdot & & & \\ \cdot & & & \\ s^{p1}\,a^1 & s^{p2}\,a^2 & \cdots & s^{pp}\,a^p \end{bmatrix} \tag{10-20}$$

where s^{KL} and a^L are each $(p \times p)$ matrices of pure trade and technical coefficients for each region, in the case of (a^L), and each pair of regions, in the case of (s^{KL}). The use of such "pure" coefficients would greatly facilitate the estimation of impacts associated with change in either production technology or transportation systems and/or rates.

Assume that, because of the construction of a navigable channel, such as the Arkansas River Project, a subset of industries in region 1 can deliver output

in all other regions at lower prices than was the case previously. It would be
expected that

$$\hat{s}_{ij}^{1L} \geqslant s_{ij}^{1L}, i, j = 1, \ldots, n; L = 2, \ldots, m \qquad (10\text{-}21)$$

and for certain interindustry, interregional combinations (i.e., some i, j, and L)

$$\hat{s}_{ij}^{1L} > s_{ij}^{1L} \qquad (10\text{-}22)$$

where $\hat{s}$ represents the interregional trade coefficient after the trade patterns
have shifted in response to the new set of economic conditions imposed by the
waterway. Inequality (10-22) amounts to an assertion that some of the industries in region 1, most likely those where output is amenable to water transportation, have captured a larger share of the national market for those
commodities.

Clearly, the delivered price of goods being shipped into the region should
be no greater than before, and, for those commodities that can be shipped by
water, these costs should be lower. Therefore, it would be expected that the
total volume of commodities, both final products and intermediate goods,
coming into the region would increase. Unlike the export trade pattern described above, in-shipment trade coefficients may be greater or less than before
the project. That is,

$$\hat{s}_{ij}^{K1} \mathrel{\substack{< \\ = \\ >}} s_{ij}^{K1}, i, j = 1, \ldots, n; K = 2, \ldots, m \qquad (10\text{-}23)$$

This is due to changes in the entire distribution system. Region 1 may have
moved out of the effective market area of one region and into the market area
of another. The latter would tend to be those that can make use of the waterway
for shipments to region 1. The direct effects of the water resource investment
in this case would be an expected increase in final demand for those industries
where output is water transportable. This change in final demand is largely
associated with increased extraregional demand, as domestic producers are able
to capture a larger share of the national market for these water transportable
outputs. Not only will there be an expansion of output of some regional
producers, there will very likely be a startup of activities (sectors) that heretofore
had not operated in the region.[i] These would probably be representatives of
those industries that were identified as water transport oriented. As suggested
above, such development may be contingent on the availability of appropriate
raw materials in the region.

---

[i]Recall that the project region in this case is an agricultural area that is urbanizing and
industrializing. In this stage of development, the area would be characterized by a specialized industry composition.

If there are economies of scale to be captured in the urban-industrial growth process, they would be expected to be present in growing sectors in this region type. If so, the technical coefficients of production would change as well as the trade coefficients.

$$\hat{a}^1_{ij} \leqslant a^1_{ij}, i,j = 1, \ldots, n \tag{10-24}$$

with, in some cases (i.e., some i and j),

$$\hat{a}^1_{ij} < a^1_{ij} \tag{10-25}$$

where $\hat{a}$ represents the technical coefficient after the investment. That is, such economies should reduce the input required per dollar of output for some intersectoral relationships within the region. Diseconomies of scale, which might arise out of increased congestion of the region's transport system, may lead to increases in some of the technical coefficients. Given the nature of the region, it is probable that economies of scale would more than offset any diseconomies.

The net developmental impacts should be an expansion of employment, population, and income in the region. Furthermore, the probability of actually stimulating regional growth, in general, may be greater for transport-oriented investment than for other types of projects. Because this region still has a large agricultural sector, there may be sizeable gains in both per capita and total income occasioned by a reallocation of labor from the agriculture sector to manufacturing employment. The latter should experience a sizeable increase following the completion of the project. Other changes may occur in the agricultural sector, where, if otherwise practical, production of those crops suitable for water transportation such as grain and soybeans may begin.

The general increase in activity will probably lead to substantial inmovement of both capital and labor. Increased labor demand in total may not be satisfied by project area residents, as some types of skilled labor will not be available in the project area. In this case, increased population, employment, and industry diversification should be consistent with an expanded range of choices for the region's producers and consumers, and, therefore, should be a reflection of true economic growth.[j]

Case 4. Irrigation Project—Agricultural Area

Of the various services provided by water investments, those associated with irrigation projects probably have the most immediate impact on the

---

[j]In this regard, further increases in size in our larger cities may not, in general, result in an expansion of the choice space for the area's residents. In fact, if such activity growth leads to increased congestion and population density, it may have the reverse effect.

project area economy. The provision of irrigation water in a previously unirrigated area may result in one or more of the following, depending on the nature of the region.

It might allow agricultural production on land that previously had been desert or marginal rangeland. Production in arid areas such as parts of Arizona, California, Texas, etc., probably would be nonexistent in the absence of low-cost irrigation water.

The addition of more water to land already under cultivation should result in increased output for given levels of other inputs; equivalently, the marginal product of water is positive when used for irrigation purposes. Clearly, there is a point beyond which the marginal product would be negative.

Increased availability of water, either for periodic irrigation on a regular basis, or to supplement rainfall during unusual dry spells (as it might be used in the Corn Belt) will allow increased flexibility in cropping patterns. Crops that heretofore had not been raised because of insufficient rainfall may now be added to the feasible set of commodities. This increased range of choice for the farmer allows him more latitude in adjusting cropping patterns to take advantage of market trends.

In areas where rainfall is generally adequate, the provision of irrigation water, as sort of an emergency reserve to be drawn upon in the event of a prolonged dry spell, would allow rather significant changes in production technology. For example, the farmer, knowing with certainty that his crops will get sufficient moisture on a regular basis, will be able to increase significantly the application of fertilizer. Without a water reserve, such increased fertilization might reduce yields if rainfall turned out to be inadequate.

Again, emphasis will be given only to the direct effects of such an investment. The indirect impacts may, in total, be greater, but techniques for estimating indirect impacts (e.g., input-output models) are well-developed and there is a sizeable body of literature describing their construction and use.

In this case, perhaps more than any of the others, the price effects are highly important. Many agricultural commodities, especially some of the low-protein feed grains, have price and income elasticities of demand which are relatively low. The former implies that, increased output can only be marketed at prices that have fallen by a greater proportion than the increase in output. For example, if the price elasticity of demand for corn is 0.5, a 20 percent increase in output would lead to a price decline of 40 percent, and a decrease in total revenue of 28 percent. The regional impacts of this decline are quite unequal. While price declines will effect producers in all regions, output increases are experienced only in the project area. Although most farmers may be worse off as a result of the project, those outside the project region will suffer the greatest declines in revenues and profits as shown in the example below. The consumer benefit from this development should be noted.

For a very small scale irrigation project, the associated revenue declines may not be an important consideration, but even for a modest project, or for a number of small projects, the possibility is very real. Too often, benefit-cost analyses for water development projects in agricultural areas have valued increased output at the going market price, without making any adjustment for the possibility of a decline in price caused by an increase in the supply function. In many cases the implicit assumption of constant prices is erroneous.

It is clear that if the project is of sufficient scale to increase total output and reduce prices even slightly, there could be rather substantial differential impacts among regions. Consider the following hypothetical example. Assume there are only two regions (A and B) producing a given agricultural commodity that will be called "corn-beans." Before the irrigation project in Region A, production, gross revenues, and income were as indicated below:

	Region A	Region B	Nation
Acres in production	100,000	100,000	200,000
Production (1000 bushels)	10,000	10,000	20,000
Price per bushel	$1.00	$1.00	$1.00
Total revenue ($000)	$10,000	$10,000	$20,000
Total costs ($000)	$6,000	$6,000	$12,000
Net income ($000)	$4,000	$4,000	$8,000

Now assume that an irrigation project is completed in Region A to provide supplemental water to area farmers who, during the course of the season buy 100,000 acre-feet at, say, $5.00 per acre-foot, and that this water, plus increased fertilizer application, enables them to increase output by 20 percent. Farmers in Region B continue to produce 10,000,000 bushels. If the price elasticity of demand for "corn-beans" is 0.5,[k] the price would have to fall to $0.80 in order to clear the market of this increased output. The net result of these changes, as summarized below, is a reduction in net income in both regions, although clearly the impact is more severe in Region B.

	Region A	Region B	Nation
Acres in production	100,000	100,000	200,000
Production (1000 bushels)	12,000	10,000	22,000
Price per bushel	$0.80	$0.80	$0.80
Total revenue ($000)	$9,600	$8,000	$17,600
Total cost ($000)	$7,000[l]	$6,000	$13,000
Net income	$2,600	$2,000	$4,600

---

[k]This assumed price elasticity approximates those estimated empirically for feed grains such as corn. See Brandow.[8]

[l]Includes $500,000 for water and $500,000 for increased fertilizer application made feasible by the availability of supplemental water.

That the price elasticity of demand for the commodity is critical in predicting the effect on net income, should be clear from examination of the following data on the relationship between the elasticity and net farm income in the two regions of our example:

Price Elasticity of Demand	Equilibrium Price of "Corn-beans"	Net Farm Income		
		Region A	Region B	Nation
2.00	0.95	4,400	3,500	7,900
1.00	0.90	3,800	3,000	6,800
0.50	0.80	2,600	2,000	4,600
0.25	0.60	200	-0-	200

The above analysis, while descriptive of a very real problem in the agricultural sector, is a little unrealistic because it was implicitly assumed that the demand function was invariant as the supply function increased. In reality, the demand functions for many agricultural commodities are increasing over time as population and incomes increase. The specification of the demand equation as quantity demanded as a function of a single variable, price, is grossly incomplete. Although demand for most agricultural products is income inelastic (i.e., $E_y < 1$), it is generally positive, implying increases in the demand function as incomes rise. Therefore, irrigation projects, if planned and timed properly, need not have the negative impacts shown in our example. One objective of irrigation investment planning should be to facilitate just enough increased supply to meet increased demand at an "equitable" price (defined as one allowing the farmer a "fair" return).

Consider the same data as in our example, except that the demand function has shifted so that 10 percent more of the commodity is demanded at all prices. In this case the price should remain unchanged.[m]

	Region A	Region B	Nation
Production (1000 bushels)	12,000	10,000	22,000
Price per bushel	$1.00	$1.00	$1.00
Total revenue ($000)	$12,000	$10,000	$22,000
Total costs ($000)	$7,000	$6,000	$13,000
Net income ($000)	$5,000	$4,000	$9,000

[m]Specification of a price maintenance objective ignores a potentially more interesting question, which is indirectly related to the change in irrigation water supply. What would the net incomes of the two regions have been without any increase in corn-bean supply, but with the ten percent increase in demand? Given price elasticities which are typical of many farm crops, this net revenue could quite conceivably have been higher without the project. In fact, we find that other input-expanding technologies tend to induce increases in supply which are considerably larger than observed increases in demand. Thus, additional increases in demand. Thus, additional increases in corn-bean supply, which result from added irrigation water supplies, can result in combined net incomes which are less than they would have been without the project.

In this case, Region *A* is better off, as net income is higher than before the project, and Region *B* is in the same position as before.

Furthermore, should an irrigation project lead to declines in total revenue and profit on one crop, there are always alternative crops that can be planted during the next season. Again, that region where the investment was made will have an advantage, because, with the supplemental water, the farmer in that region will tend to have a greater range of choice in crop selection than would farmers in neighboring, but unirrigated, areas.

The relevant point is that the net impacts of an irrigation project can be positive or negative, in terms of the effect on farm income, depending on the price and income elasticities of demand for the commodity (or commodities) being produced, the secular shift in the demand function, the increase in output caused by the availability of irrigation water, the possibility of switching to other crops, etc. In summary, it is a rather complex problem that requires very thorough analysis of a number of factors. One thing is clear, however; merely multiplying an estimate of increased production by the going market price is a very poor estimate of the true primary benefits of an irrigation project.

Notes

1. Charles L. Leven, ed., *Development Benefits of Water Resource Investments,* a report submitted to the U.S. Army Corps of Engineers, Institute for Water Resources (Springfield, Virginia: Clearinghouse for Federal Scientific and Technical Information, November 1969).
2. *Ibid.*
3. George S. Tolley, ed., *Estimation of First Round and Selected Subsequent Income Effects of Water Resources Investment,* a report submitted to the U.S. Army Corps of Engineers, Institute for Water Resources (Springfield, Virginia: Clearinghouse for Federal Scientific and Technical Information, February 1970).
4. Barge and Towing Industry Association, *United for Action* (Washington, D.C.: American Waterways Operations, May, 1971) p. 3.
5. T.E. Nichols, "Transportation and Regional Development in Agriculture," *American Journal of Agricultural Economics*, LI, 5 (December, 1969) 1455–63.
6. Charles L. Leven and R.B. Read, *A River, A Region and A Research Problem*, a report submitted to the U.S. Army Corps of Engineers, Institute for Water Resources, Alexandria, Virginia, March, 1971.
7. *Ibid.*, p. 157.
8. G.E. Brandow, *Inter-Relations Among Demands for Farm Products and Implications for Control of Market Supply* (University Park: Agricultural Experiment Station, College of Agriculture, Pennsylvania State University, August 1961).

11 Summary and Conclusions

The overall purpose of this book has been to demonstrate how the tools of economics, operations research, and statistics can be brought to bear on questions relative to the role that water-oriented investment might play in the development of a regional economy.[a] This was done in three major parts. The first was a framework for the economic analysis, the second on the role of water resource investment in regional growth, and the third on an accounting framework for the analysis. In the first part, the chapters were devoted to consideration of appropriate area delineation for investment planning; regional growth theory; and the appropriate measures to be used in accounting for economic growth.

Most economic analyses of water resource investment have been done on regions which were delineated without economic orientation. Yet much of the analysis for justification of projects is on the basis of economic relationships. Unfortunately, when regions are delineated on a strictly hydrologic basis, the economic effects spill over into adjacent basins. This presents only minor problems so long as the evaluation of project impacts is restricted to the national viewpoint. But if regional impacts are important, then a regional context is needed which enables a more accurate and realistic assessment of these impacts. Flows of people and flows of economic activity among these regions may be a more appropriate base for delineation than flows of water. Thus, it is recommended that an FEA (functional economic area) delineation be used. These units may be adapted to hydrologic units by careful aggregation so that the economic interrelationships as well as hydrologic measurements can be analyzed. Stability of projections and adequate tracing of regional economic impacts depends on this approach.

In Chapter 3, the state of regional growth theory was critically reviewed. There it was shown that the commonly-used export-base model of growth is inadequate for understanding the growth process. The shortcomings of this method can perhaps best be seen by considering the relationships among regions. If a region is to export more and more in order to grow, it must find another region willing to import. The idea of regions growing bigger and bigger only to supply each other with more and more exports obviously overlooks the possibility of increasing internal activities to do the same thing. Improvement

---

[a]Although the focus here has been on water resource investment specifically, the analysis has direct application to a broad range of public investment activities.

163

in the quality of factors of production is an important determinant of regional growth. It has been shown that a large portion of regional growth has resulted from improvement in factor quality and better allocation of resources. Thus, it is likely that growth in export and residentiary industries is simultaneously determined, rather than being in an independent-dependent relationship as suggested by export base analyses.

Chapter 4 noted that the appropriate measurement of economic growth is at least as important as the theoretical explanation for its occurrence. Traditionally, growth has often been accepted as a goal for its own sake. Recently, this view has been subject to question and a much broader view of the well-being of people appears to have emerged. In the past, indicators used to evaluate regional development have been analogous to national income account measures, especially gross national product. While these indicators have deficiencies in a national context, they are even less appropriate for a region. Failure to account for capital depreciation such as in machinery, highways, water facilities, and others is a serious omission. A concept analogous to Net National Product is more appropriate. But even these measures of output still fail to assess the important changes in measures of factor productivity and stocks of resources and wealth induced by growth. Also, many of the negative effects on output and quality of inputs are not incorporated into the indicators. The folly of adding into the indicators wages and other expenditures for cleaning up pollution or overcoming other external damages, while the damages themselves are not subtracted from the income indicators, has been cited. Most forms of economic production produce "good" commodities and "bad" commodities. A realistic accounting requires a netting out. These external effects may be positive or negative, and because they almost never enter into market transactions, they must be added to or subtracted from income estimates if the full impact of growth is to be accurately assessed and evaluated. If demand for a product is less than perfectly elastic (almost universally the case), then expansion will produce a price effect which will negate at least part of the value of the increase in output within the region, and will produce a negative offset for producing areas outside the region.

Frequently, specific investment projects are assumed to be justified because they purportedly are the only acceptable way of achieving more desirable distribution of welfare. But, to be rigorous, a complete analysis of both efficiency and equity impacts for a project should be made. If the efficiency test is passed, then costs of an optimal redistribution program should be added if the project distribution effects are substantial. On the other hand, if a project is designed for effectuating desirable income redistribution objectives, but fails the efficiency test, it must be demonstrated before project approval that alternative means of redistributing income are even more inefficient.

The second part of the book looked specifically at the relationship between water resource development and regional growth. It was hypothestized that water investment could influence growth in one or more of the following ways: alleviating scarcities which constrain production levels; increasing water inputs may increase marginal productivity and returns to other factors including labor; and introducing water or additional water might change optimal techniques of production so that the production function may shift upward to increase output per unit of input. On closer analysis, however, it appears that water is a relatively unimportant input in many nonagricultural industries. Generally, water and related inputs (e.g., hydroelectric power) account for a small part of total production costs, and, therefore, would tend to be of little consequence in the industrial location decision. Water must be available for use, but its price is not an important factor compared to more costly items like labor. The review of the literature on this subject confirms this conclusion. The choice of the broad (macro) location is based primarily on market or demand consideration and the microlocation decision is based on cost factors of which water cost is one of the less important. However, there are manufacturing sectors where water inputs are relatively important, and, of course, they are very significant in irrigated agriculture. In such sectors, water investment may have a positive impact on economic growth.

In Chapter 6, a possible sequence of development impacts was outlined. Briefly summarized, this sequence was: (1) resource development (investment for creation of regional activity potential); (2) changes in relative factor productivities (inter- and intraregional changes in productivity and cost); (3) broadening the range of producer and consumer choice (higher incomes, more jobs, recreation, lower cost of producers); (4) intra- and interregional movement of productive facilities and people (reaction of resource owners to expanded range of choice which leads to the mutual interaction of migration and productive capacity); (5) immediate forward and backward linkage effects (multiple income effects on retail, wholesale and service sectors—the amount of effect depends on the "leakages" in the area); and (6) second order impacts associated with scale economies, agglomeration and attainment of minimum threshold levels of activity.

The last part of the book was devoted to a review of the techniques that can be used to predict and account for the economic impacts associated with water resource investment. In Chapter 8, the earlier arguments on measures of growth, regional delineation, and regional growth theory were brought together to provide a framework to assess the effects of an array of different kinds of water projects or regions of various kinds. The analysis concentrated on the economic services provided by a project, although physical nature of construction is also of some concern. A planning framework for a project should include: economic services provided; physical characteristics and construction outlays; and development benefits, especially relative to the size of the economy.

Regional investment and regional development must be considered at least partly from a national perspective (assuming at least partial federal funding) and both direct and indirect effects must be estimated. The format for assessment of development impacts deals with various kinds of indicators of the impacts of each kind of service generated by each of the several kinds of investments in each of the many regions. The first step is simply a listing of the development impacts cross-classified by investment type, by type of services provided by type of region. The next step is a detailed analysis of each of the nonzero (positive or negative) elements in this classification. This step involves analysis of income, employment by sector, urbanization, per capita income, employment rate and environmental effects for each of several FEA's which make up a region, and a summation of all of these to a region total. The next step is summation of all of these regional effects to a national total for each indicator. Admittedly, this is a highly idealized situation such that complete, accurate quantification of each indicator in every region may not be possible, but, at least qualitative judgments are suggested by the complete framework.

Implicit in the discussion of empirical techniques for predicting economic impacts is the recognition that no one tool can be appropriately applied in every situation. The conceptual basis for most of these techniques is the production function which is the real "link" between the physical and economic systems which is so critical in water resource analysis. Without these basic data, none of the techniques can be successfully operated. The models discussed are all designed to represent or "simulate" some parts of the real world. Some operate under assumed optimizing behavior and some do not. The appropriateness of any one or combination of techniques depends on the particular problem at hand. Input-output, linear programming, econometric modeling, and simulation have all been successfully applied in research on water resource investments. However, improvements in public investment feasibility analysis will require expansion of the range of quantitative tools and improvement in the quality of their application.

What then can one conclude from this synthesis? One point is quite clear—the very general question, "Does water resource development stimulate regional economic growth?," is not amenable to a simple yes or no answer. Under some circumstances, in some regions, there exist a class of investments that will expand the rate of economic activity. Under other circumstances, the same project may have little or no effect on the regional economy in question. Although, in some situations, a case-by-case approach must be used, general applications might be drawn and predictions made on the basis of previous analyses of region-investment type combinations.

It is also obvious that regional development is multidimensional with water resources playing only one part, and, in some cases, a relatively small one. Thus, if regional economic development is a primary objective, water resource investment probably should be made in combination with other types of public investment such as manpower development and training, highway construction and improvements, urban renewal, etc.

Furthermore, there may be undesirable kinds of development following the installation of certain kinds of water investment. If environmental objectives are of great importance, increased central control of the type of development that can take place in areas surrounding the water resource may be needed. Often, short-run monetary considerations dominate the thinking of local business and political interests, sometimes resulting in development with little long-run potential. Or, the development may be inconsistent with environmental objectives. As federal monies are typically involved in the investment, and since state and local agencies are involved financially and otherwise, it would seem logical to have more control over the secondary types of development around the primary investment. Perhaps local, state, and federal agencies should be given increased control over the way development should proceed.

Although not directly a part of the investment-economic growth question, another argument is summarized at this point. A major obstacle to the efficient allocation of resources is the commonly-held notion that the "special" nature of the resource water (which apparently stems from its life-giving qualities) insulates development planning from considerations of thorough economic analysis that would require that the national efficiency criterion be met before an investment is made. Some advocates of this principle would prefer to justify water development on emotional or intuitive grounds that such investment is inherently good. The position taken in this book is that water, admittedly possessing life-giving qualities, should be treated essentially the same as other resources. That is, pricing and investment actions should be preceded by solid economic evaluation.

Similarly, another practice common to water resource planning which is extremely damaging is the use of a set of water requirements rather than an economic demand function. Unfortunately, society has treated the water resource in a highly emotional and inconsistent way. Allegations that a region is suffering from a "shortage" of water would often fail to stand up under a rational investigation based on sound economic principles. To assume that some projected amount of water "need" must be met even if its marginal value is, in fact, very low impedes the possibility of substituting plentiful resources for relatively scarce water. This promotes excessive investment in water resources, excessive rates of water use, and underutilization of other resources. The most appropriate factors to consider in setting administrative prices are: (1) the demand schedule for water in various uses (value decreases at higher rates of use—decreasing marginal value productivity or decreasing marginal utility); (2) the supply schedule for water to be delivered to various uses (successively larger quantities of water are usually more expensive to provide— increasing marginal costs); and, of a second order of importance, (3) equity to the purchasers.

Finally, it is clear that there is a need for additional empirical research on effects of water investment on economic growth. That which has been done still leaves a number of questions unanswered and hypotheses untested. More case studies of the regional economic impacts of specific projects are needed, especially those comparing development in the project area to that in a similar control area which has had no such investment. (The studies outlined in Chapter 10 are intended to be indicative only, and need thorough empirical testing.) Empirical research should also be undertaken to determine if there are developmental threshold levels associated with different project sizes and types. While consideration and compensation are given to those who suffer losses from water investments (e.g., those individuals who have to give up their homes and property because it will be inundated by a reservoir), generally there is no compensation paid by those who benefit from the project. This is especially true for landowners who will reap windfall gains by owning property on or near the water resource that is created or improved. Essentially, this is the case of an externality that might be internalized by social ownership of the property or through appropriate tax policies. The problem is that some of the growth or development accrues to particular individuals which make the distribution effects undesirable. More research is needed on the extent of this problem and the means to overcome it.

Index

About the Authors

W. Cris Lewis is a member of the Economics faculty at Utah State University. He received the Ph.D. from Iowa State University and was formerly on the faculty of the University of Oklahoma. He has published a number of articles in the field of urban-regional economics, and has served as a consultant to public agencies and private industry.

Jay C. Andersen is on the Economics faculty at Utah State University. He received the Ph.D. from Iowa State University. He was formerly with the Economics Research Service, U.S. Department of Agriculture. He has published many articles in agricultural and regional economics and has been a consultant to several public and private groups on water resource development problems.

Herbert H. Fullerton is assistant professor of Agricultural Economics in the Economics Department of Utah State University. The focus for his research and several publications is in the area of public resource policy, with emphasis on water and water related activities and public lands.

B. Delworth Gardner is Professor and Head of the Economics Department at Utah State University. He received the Ph.D. from the University of Chicago in 1960, and has served on the faculty at Colorado State University and Brigham Young University. He was a Visiting Professor of the University of California, Berkeley, and a Visiting Scholar at Resources for the Future. He has published numerous articles in the fields of Agricultural and Resource Economics.